Letterland™

EARLY YEARS

HANDBOOK

by Judy Manson and Mark Wendon

Published by Collins Educational
An imprint of HarperCollinsPublishers Ltd
77-85 Fulham Palace Road
London W6 8JB

The HarperCollins website address is:
www.fireandwater.com

First published by Letterland Ltd 1995

This edition published 1997 by Collins Educational

Reprinted 1997, 1999 (twice)

ISBN 0 00 303320 1

British Library Cataloguing in Publication Data
A catalogue record for this book is available from the British Library.

Photographs by Martin Sookias
Design by Sally Boothroyd
Cover design by Sylvia Kwan
Pictogram colouring by Gina Hart
Origination by Applescan Reproductions Plc.
Printed by printing Express Ltd, Hong Kong

Acknowledgements
The authors and publishers would like to thank the following:
The staff and children at Allfarthing Primary School, Earlsfield, London
for their help with the photographs
The staff and children at the Caterpillar Nursery, Balham, London for
their help with the photographs
The staff and children at Charlbury Primary School, Charlbury,
Oxfordshire for their help with the photographs
The staff and children at Flora Garden School, Hammersmith, London
for their help with the photographs
Sue Leverton for her teaching advice

Letterland™

EARLY YEARS

HANDBOOK

by Judy Manson and Mark Wendon

Educational consultant: Lyn Wendon

Collins Educational

An imprint of HarperCollinsPublishers

Contents

Foreword

Nurseries and reception classes aim to create a place where learning can take place naturally and without pressure. Letterland is ideally suited to this environment. That's why more and more people have been asking for guidance on using Letterland in nurseries and in reception classes. This handbook is the result!

Since the handbook is for very young children, it introduces Letterland very simply. It lays the foundation for reading. It teaches letter shape and sound recognition and it establishes correct letter formation, while at the same time engendering a delight in language and a delight in learning. Letterland is a place to enjoy, both for young and old.

Lyn Wendon

Introduction to Letterland

Teaching children to read and write can be a formidable task. Letterland uses entertaining stories to teach letter behaviour in ways that even very young children can understand and enjoy. In place of meaningless rules and exceptions, Letterland characters like Annie Apple and Bouncy Ben make children instantly aware of the way letters look and sound.

Take the letter **h**. At first sight it is simply a random mark for a young child. There are no clues in the letter's shape or name ('aitch') to the sound it makes in words. But brought to life as the 'Hairy Hat Man', his body and his name become instant clues to the correct shape and sound.

Similarly, when the capital **H** is presented as the same Hairy Hat Man doing a handstand (because he is so excited at starting a sentence or a name), the link between **h** and **H** becomes instantly memorable.
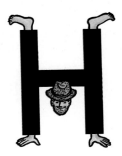

Most methods of teaching the alphabet provide no link to changes in letter sounds in combinations like **sh** and **ch**. In Letterland, by contrast, these new sounds are easily explained in stories about how the Hairy Hat Man and his Letterland friends behave when they meet each other in words.

Letterland combinations are not covered in this handbook, but at the next stage in the *Programme One Teacher's Guide*. However, as you introduce the alphabet with this handbook you can be confident that nothing you teach will have to be unlearnt later. You will be giving your children an excellent foundation on which you or others can build the full structure of reading and writing skills.

In Letterland, children not only hear about letters, but they experience them as well! They can dress up as the Letterland characters themselves and act out their behaviour in little plays. They can recreate them in art and craft, they can sing songs about them and retell stories about them in their own words. The result is a unique multi-sensory experience of the alphabet and a very memorable introduction to the world of print.

The Letterland Early Years Programme

The materials

Essential

☆ *Letterland Early Years Handbook*
☆ *Letterland Early Years Cassette*
☆ *Letterland ABC Book*
☆ *Letterland Class Wall Frieze*
☆ *Letterland Handwriting Songs Cassette*
☆ *Letterland Alphabet Songs Cassette*

(**Note** The above materials will be used throughout the *Early Years Handbook* for each Letterland character, so they are not listed under the **What you need** section on individual letter pages.)

Highly recommended

☆ *Letterland Early Years Workbooks 1-4*
☆ *Letterland Early Years Big Picture Code Cards*
☆ *Letterland Lower Case Pictogram Copymasters*
☆ *Letterland Early Years Handwriting Copymasters*
☆ *Letterland An Alphabet of Rhymes Book*

Notes about the materials

Early Years Handbook

This handbook has been specially written for teachers and pre-school leaders who wish to introduce Letterland to their children. It provides guidance on how to introduce all the Letterland characters including the Vowel Men (long vowels) and lots of practical ideas for follow-up activities and discussion.

A double-page spread is devoted to every Letterland character. The first page of each spread has detailed notes on how to introduce each letter, how to teach the sound it makes in words, how to write it correctly and how to explain the varying capital letter shapes. The second page is packed with follow-up suggestions of things you may like to do and talk about to provide reinforcement for each letter. Each spread also includes a tape transcript of the *Early Years Cassette* as a useful model for you to follow.

Suggestions for activities you can do with the children

Points for discussion

Letterland materials (other than the core materials) which are useful for teaching this particular Letterland character

The Letterland explanation for the capital letter pictogram

Example words beginning with that character's sound

The Letterland explanation for the long vowel sound

Examples of long vowel words

The transcript of the *Early Years Cassette* for each Letterland character

Although this handbook is laid out in alphabetical order, you may wish to choose a teaching order to complement your own programme. At the Early Years level, focusing on one letter each week generally seems to work well, but be ready to talk about other pictogram characters if asked. If some children are already familiar with the characters through family or friends, they will still enjoy the repetition and may even help other children. Being able to write his or her own name is an important skill in a child's early development, so as soon as it arises, tell each child which Letterland characters go together to make up their name. (See also **Long vowels** on page 15.)

Early Years Cassette

The cassette is divided into two sessions and follows a similar pattern for each Letterland character: an introduction to the character followed by the character's sound and shape. The two sessions should ideally be presented on two separate days.

The *Early Years Cassette* is not intended for playing to the children. The purpose of the cassette is to provide an example of a teaching style you may like to adopt. It will also help you to pronounce the letter sounds correctly. A transcript of the cassette for each letter is provided on the relevant letter page in this handbook. Use your own wording to cover the content, and don't worry if you leave points out. Letterland is intended to be flexible.

ABC Book

You will be using the illustrations in the *ABC Book* throughout this handbook to introduce each new Letterland character, but it is better to save the written text for parents and children to share at home. Instead, talk about the pictures using the *Early Years Cassette* as a guide for what to say.

Class Wall Frieze

Mount the frieze on the wall at a comfortable height for the children. They will need to be able to touch the various Letterland characters with ease and trace over them with their fingers.

Handwriting Songs Cassette

The *Handwriting Songs Cassette* provides a fun way of learning how to form all 26 letter shapes with the help of the Letterland characters. The words to these songs are on each letter page and are laid out in full on page 76 of this handbook. They are also featured in the *Early Years Handwriting Copymasters* (see opposite).

Alphabet Songs Cassette

The *Alphabet Songs Cassette* is intended to help children pronounce all the letter sounds correctly. Each song is sung to the tune of a well-known nursery rhyme. The words for these can be found on page 72 of this handbook.

Early Years Workbooks 1-4

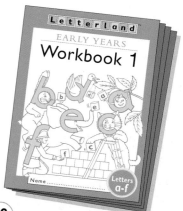

These workbooks give children further practice in writing all the letter shapes and familiarise them with words beginning with their sounds.

For every Letterland character there are a minimum of two workbook pages. The first page in each case focuses on the shape of the letter, so that children start to distinguish one letter from another. The second page focuses on the sound it makes in words. For every character there is also a more open-ended extension activity which encourages children to think about the letter sound in other contexts.

Early Years Big Picture Code Cards

The *Early Years Big Picture Code Cards* were specially produced with Early Years children in mind. They consist of 46 large, easy-to-handle cards comprising all the lower case Letterland characters. Five long vowel (Vowel Men) cards are also provided, as well as extra short vowel cards and some extra consonants. In each case one side shows the pictogram letter and on the reverse is the plain letter shape, so that you can, with a flick of the wrist, help with the transition to plain letter identification. Examples of words beginning with each letter sound are also provided on the backs of the cards.

These cards are particularly useful for finger tracing letter shapes, for revising sounds learnt so far, and for building simple words. Further ideas for their usage are provided with the cards themselves.

Lower Case Pictogram Copymasters

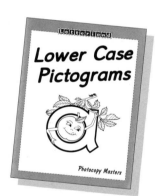

Photocopiable sheets are available for all 26 lower case or small letters. Children can practise the correct handwriting strokes within the hollow letters and can colour in the Letterland characters. Full instructions are provided with the copymasters.

Early Years Handwriting Copymasters

The *Early Years Handwriting Copymasters* consist of 48 pages of pattern and letter practice for all 26 lower case letter shapes. Each Letterland character has its own pattern practice page, and the remaining copymasters provide practice in correct letter formation, with the help of the appropriate handwriting verse. Full instructions are provided with the copymasters.

An Alphabet of Rhymes Book

An Alphabet of Rhymes Book is strongly recommended to support your Letterland teaching. It is only referred to in this handbook for certain Letterland characters, but if available, choose any rhyme you feel is suitable as part of your **Things to talk about** options.

Teaching with Letterland

The 'journey to Letterland'

On your first 'journey to Letterland' with the children, introduce the idea of Letterland by reading them the text on page 6 of the *ABC Book*. In subsequent sessions, start with a pretend 'journey to Letterland' routine if time allows. Let children help you to decide how to get there. You may like to mime getting into a bus, train or plane. The children could also close their eyes for a few moments and then open them to arrive in Letterland.

Teaching each alphabet letter

Having 'arrived in Letterland', you will then be ready to introduce the first Letterland character to the children. **Session 1** from the *Early Years Cassette* or the transcript of the text in this handbook will help you to do this. The second part of the transcript (**Session 2**), which covers the shape and sound of the Letterland character, should be used a day or two after **Session 1**. This gives children time to absorb and then recall the information.

The **Things to do** section will then provide you with numerous ideas for possible follow-up activities. Discussion topics are provided in the **Things to talk about** section. Many of these ideas are applicable to several of the letters. Further general activity suggestions are also given on page 16 under **Further ideas.**

Letter shapes

Letterland pictograms act as signposts orientating a child's eyes in the 'Reading Direction'. When teaching letter shapes, it is important to remember that the Reading Direction is always from a child's left to right. If you are facing the class it will be reversed for you, so take care that you don't accidentally demonstrate a letter stroke in reverse. Instead, half turn your back so that you are facing the same way as the children while you make the stroke. Encourage children to finger trace the picture-coded letters on the *Early Years Big Picture Code Cards* or on the *ABC Book*. By following the shape with their finger, they are more likely to make it correctly when they come to use a pencil.

The basis of good handwriting is correct pencil grip and correct letter formation. Make sure the children know the correct grip from the start. Once established, a poor grip can very easily become a life-time habit.

Good relaxed grip   Poor, tense grip

Gently encourage children to practise the correct grip until they get it right. With children who have not yet established which hand to use, simply place the crayon or pencil between both hands and leave the choice to them.

left-handed   right-handed

pencil position   page position   pencil position   page position

If a child forms a letter incorrectly, do gently intervene. For example, when a child mistakenly writes his or her **e**'s with a clockwise circle and then breaks the stroke, you could say, 'Eddy Elephant likes you to stroke across his headband *first*, and *end* with his trunk. Let's practise it with one line all the way round.' You may well be preventing that child from developing a permanent bad habit.

Handwriting practice is available on the *Lower Case Pictogram Copymasters,* the *Early Years Handwriting Copymasters* and the *Early Years Workbooks*. Pattern practice prior to letter formation is also included on the *Early Years Handwriting Copymasters*. Listening to and singing along with the *Handwriting Songs Cassette* is also an enjoyable way to help children remember how to form letter shapes. The full lyrics to these songs are available on page 76 of this handbook.

The Letterland stories, songs and activities all contribute to learning correct letter formation effortlessly. Remember that the correct sequence of strokes is more important than tidiness at this stage.

Letter names and sounds

To begin with, always refer to letters by their Letterland names*, for example, 'Clever Cat' and not 'cee'. Traditional letter names like 'cee, aitch, em, cue, are, double-u, why' are confusing because they do not match the sounds that letters make in words. By contrast, by *starting* to say any Letterland character's name, the child can rely on having just said that letter's correct sound.

A useful way to practise isolating the letter sound from the character name is to use hand signals. Ask the children to start to say the Letterland character's name very slowly. For instance, for Munching Mike, they say 'Mmm...' when you hold your hand up, opened wide.

Close your hand as the signal for the children to close their mouths and be silent.

The Letterland *Alphabet Songs* are also useful for ensuring that children pronounce all the letter sounds correctly. The lyrics to these can be found on pages 72 of this handbook and the songs are available on cassette (see page 10).

Capital letters

Letterland presents both lower case and capital letter shapes on the *Class Wall Frieze*. While your focus will be on the lower case letter shapes, because these are the shapes used most in writing, each child should learn to recognise and write the capital letter that starts his or her name. A helpful guideline when teaching how to write any of these capital letter shapes is, 'Always start at the top.'

Any other capitals the children learn will be interesting for them to know and fun to recognise on signs, etc., but at this stage, learning to write capital letters should take lower priority than learning to recognise and write the lower case letter shapes.

*If, for whatever reason, you have a problem using one or more of the Letterlanders' names, for example, because you have a boy called Nick in your group, feel free to change 'Naughty Nick' to 'Noisy Nick' or 'Nice Nick'. Do, however, postpone the confusing alphabet names during the early stages of learning to read and write.

Long vowels

The first sounds that children need to know for the five vowels, **a, e, i, o** and **u**, are the short vowel sounds, represented in Letterland by Annie Apple, Eddy Elephant, Impy Ink, Oscar Orange and Uppy Umbrella.

Many words, however, including children's own names, often contain long vowels. By personifying the long vowels as Vowel Men (the only people in Letterland who ever say their alphabet names in words), Letterland helps children to understand that each of these five vowel letter shapes actually has two different sounds.

The Vowel Men are namely Mr A (the Apron Man), Mr E (the Easy Magic Man), Mr I (the Ice Cream Man), Mr O (the Old Man) and Mr U (the Uniform Man). By seeing and even dressing up as both long and short vowels, and by comparing them on the *Early Years Big Picture Code Cards*, the children will improve their understanding of this dual function of the five vowels.

The children will also see the Vowel Men on the *Class Wall Frieze*. This gives you an opening to talk briefly about each of them, preparing the way for more emphasis on long vowels later. However, from the outset you may have an **A**my, **Si**mon, **Jo**seph, etc. in your class, or children of other nationalities with long vowels in their names. To them you can say, 'Your name is special because Mr A himself appears in it instead of Annie Apple', etc.

Parental involvement

Parents are becoming increasingly interested in how their children learn to read. Literacy skills are the foundation of a child's future attainment, so it is a great help to children when parents and teachers join together to support their reading, writing and spelling. Page 80 sets out some guidelines for parents. You may like to photocopy this page and give it to the parents, or use it as a starting point to write your own information sheet for them. A 'who's who' of Letterland is also available on pages 78-9.*

Your own ideas

This handbook is just intended to help you get started. You will soon develop your own style and ideas for appropriate activities. You may like to note them in the margin, or at the back of the guide. This will help you and your colleagues to remember and re-use good ideas.

* **Please note:** The 'who's who' of Letterland (on pages 78-9) can be photocopied only to inform parents in your school about Letterland and are not for re-sale or for commercial exploitation.

Further ideas

As soon as the children have 'met' several of the Letterland characters, opportunities arise to introduce the characters into general activities. The possibilities are endless, but here are a number of suggestions.

Display area

Collect pictures and objects beginning with the current letter. Where time allows, make a really big collage or painting of the pictogram character. It will provide an eye-catching focus on the initial sound which is common to all the pictures and objects collected around it.

Tiny object collection

Make a long row of Letterland letters under which children can place small items beginning with each letter sound, e.g. (cardboard) arrow, button, conker, (tiny toy) dog, egg-shell, etc. (Where objects are difficult to find, you can draw them or use pictures.) Remove the objects and assign specific children to re-allocate them. This activity can provide a useful form of revision of both letter sounds and the alphabet sequence.

Dressing up

Add steadily to a 'Clever Cat's Costume Box' by collecting or making props, such as a toy fireman's helmet, animal ears, beards and a king's crown (see the photographs on each character spread for further ideas). Each new Letterland prop will add to the possibilities of Letterland-related activities in free play. Parents might enjoy being enlisted to sew or create these props.

Miming without props

Once the children are familiar with a few of the Letterland characters, ask one or more children to say the sound or mime the behaviour of a letter of their choice. The other children then have to guess who they are. Repeat this activity as they become familiar with more letters.

Painting a–z

Pencil in the letters, big and bold, as guidelines for children's paintings. They can go over them in paint and add the pictogram details. Keep their letter paintings and use them later on to build three-letter words.

Photographic a–z

Take photographs of the children pretending to be all the different Letterland characters. They could be holding or wearing *Early Years Big Picture Code Cards* and/or wearing appropriate items from 'Clever Cat's Costume Box' (see **Dressing up** on page 17). Put all the photos into an album in alphabetical order for use as a unique class ABC, as well as for amusement.

Story-telling

Start a story which takes place in Letterland. For example, 'One day after work, Fireman Fred decided to go fishing. On his way to the river he met...?' Children then supply the next words. Help them, if necessary, using alliterative words (see the example words on the relevant letter page) or with whatever other ideas come to mind. Their contributions need not include words beginning with a particular sound. The aim here is to help them to develop story-telling techniques, and to contribute parts to a whole story.

Stories by older children

Try contacting a local primary school that uses Letterland. Their children might like to write and illustrate stories about the Letterlanders for your Early Years group. This can have very positive benefits for all concerned. Your children will love sharing Letterland with older children. The older children, in turn, will be motivated to write clearly, add appropriate illustrations and present their stories attractively.

Letter spotting

The first time children recognise a letter
in their environment, it is like seeing
a friendly face in a crowd. Provide
opportunities for children to share
what they have seen. Encourage
more 'letter spotting'.

Fund-raising

Parents can run Letterland stalls at
fund-raising events, for example, a
'Clever Cat's Crafts Stall' or a 'Hairy
Hat Man's Hot Dog Stall'. They may
even enjoy impersonating Letterland
characters, thereby helping to make
any fund-raising event a bit
different!

Reading labels

By labelling items around the room, you convey the fact that
spoken words can also be written. Encourage children to read
labels, even if at this stage they can only 'read' them by knowing
their place on the wall. No Early Years children should be
pressured, however, to learn lots of 'sight words'. At this age,
their memory for sight words is often short-lived.

Revision

At the end of the week talk about the activities done to make
sure the children realise their relevance to the letter they are
learning. For instance, ask, 'Why did we play that Leaping up
game and paint a lighthouse and write letters and make little
lambs and put labels on things? Yes, because all those things
start with Lucy Lamp Lady's sound!'

Annie Apple

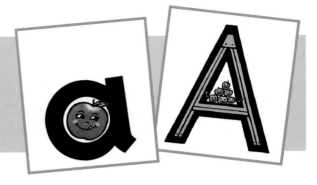

Objectives

To teach the letter shapes for **a** and **A** and the short vowel sound 'ă...', and to introduce the long vowel sound 'ā...'.

What you need

Letterland materials

☆ *Early Years Big Picture Code Cards*:
   Annie Apple and Mr A
☆ *Lower Case Pictogram Copymasters*: **a**
☆ *Early Years Handwriting Copymasters*: 1 and 27
☆ *Early Years Workbook 1*: pages 2-5

Other materials

☆ Large cardboard or paper arrows
☆ Apple shapes or templates
☆ Apples
☆ Pictures of trees

Teaching suggestions

Introducing Annie Apple

Show the children the picture of Annie Apple on page 9 of the *ABC Book* and introduce her using **Session 1** from the *Early Years Cassette* as a guide for what to say. The transcript of this cassette is also provided opposite. Invite children to find and touch Annie Apple on the *Class Wall Frieze*.

Annie Apple's letter shape

After **Session 2**, the following handwriting verse, chanted or sung as on the *Handwriting Songs Cassette*, will help in teaching Annie Apple's letter shape:

   At the leaf begin. Go round the apple this way.
   Then add a line down, so Annie won't roll away.

The lyrics for all the Handwriting Songs are available on page 76 of this book.
Invite one or more children to finger trace Annie's letter shape on the *ABC Book* or on both sides of the *Early Years Big Picture Code Cards*.

Annie Apple's sound

Remind yourself of the correct pronunciation of 'ă...' by listening to it on the *Early Years Cassette*. To be sure that the children are saying the 'ă...' sound correctly, ask them to watch as you say 'A... for Annie Apple', then ask them to reproduce just the 'ă...' sound. Annie Apple's song on the *Alphabet Songs Cassette* is also a fun way of helping both you and the children to pronounce the short 'ă...' sound correctly. The words to this song are on page 72 of this book.

   The box below provides a selection of words beginning with Annie Apple's sound. Encourage children to suggest words of their own beginning with her sound.

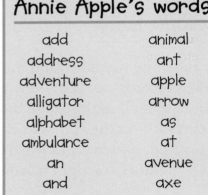

Annie Apple's words

add	animal
address	ant
adventure	apple
alligator	arrow
alphabet	as
ambulance	at
an	avenue
and	axe

Early Years Cassette transcript

Session 1: Introducing Annie Apple

I can see an **a**pple on this page. This **a**pple is *very* special. That's because she's a *Letterland* **a**pple. Can you see her smiling face *inside* her letter? She's got a *lovely* name. Her name is **A**nnie **A**pple. Can you say that? **A**nnie **A**pple.

   Can you see lots of other **a**pples here? These are all her friends who live with her on **A**pple Tree **A**venue. **A**pple Tree **A**venue leads the way to the Letterland castle.

   Can you see the **a**rrows, pointing the way to the castle? How many **a**rrows can you find on the road? One, two, three. Oh, and there's a pile of

Things to do

✿ **Arrow trail** Before the children arrive, lay a trail of large cardboard or paper arrows for them to follow, perhaps to find Annie Apple on the *Class Wall Frieze* or in the *ABC Book*.

✿ **Apple tree** Make apple templates for the children to draw round, colour in or paint. Help to cut them out and display them on a paper cut-out apple tree.

✿ **Apple printing** Cut apples across horizontally to show the 'star' pattern inside and then make apple patterns with them by pressing them on to sponges full of paint.

✿ **Follow the arrow** Make a large cardboard arrow and play 'Follow the arrow'. While pointing the arrow to the left, right, backwards, forwards or downwards, say 'Annie Apple says "Move this way."' The children then move in the right direction. (For downwards, the children will need to crouch down.)

✿ **Animals** Let the children draw animals beginning with Annie Apple's sound, e.g. an alligator, ant or antelope. If they want to, they could draw their own 'amazing animal'. Display the animals near the apple tree (see above).

✿ **Further practice** For extra practice of the letter shape, use the following materials:
– *Lower Case Pictogram Copymasters*: **a**
– *Early Years Handwriting Copymasters*: 1 and 27.
For consolidation of both letter shape and sound use:
– *Early Years Workbook 1*, pages 2-5.
See pages 10-11 for further information on these products.

Things to talk about

✿ **Alphabet** Explain the meaning of the word **alphabet**, pointing to all the letters on the *Class Wall Frieze*. Draw attention to **b**, **c**, **d** and **e** and say that they are all 'alphabet animals'.

✿ **Apple pips** Using apple pips and pictures of trees, talk about how a tiny seed grows into a big tree to give us many more apples.

Explaining the capital A shape

In Letterland, the capital A shapes are called Applestands, made by Mr A for his talking apples. The apples sit there while they say 'ă…' at the start of important words, such as names like Anne, Andrew, etc., while Mr A appears beside his Applestand in names like Amy and Adrian (see below).

Introducing Mr A, the Apron Man

Show the children the picture of Mr A, the Apron Man, on either the *Class Wall Frieze* or on the *Early Years Big Picture Code Cards*. Explain that Mr A is the man who takes care of Annie Apple and all her apple friends. At special times he appears in words instead of Annie Apple and says his name, 'ā…' as in **apron**.

Mr A's words
acorn
age
April
apron

apples in an **a**rrow shape as well.

Let's wave goodbye to **A**nnie **A**pple. We'll visit her again another day. Bye, bye, **A**nnie **A**pple.

Session 2: Annie Apple's shape and sound
Who knows the name of this happy-looking **a**pple? It's **A**nnie **A**pple. Look at her smiling face inside her letter. What colour is her letter? It's light green.

Do you know what sound **A**nnie **A**pple makes when she goes into a word? Listen, **A**nnie **A**pple says, 'ă…, ă…'. Can you say it with me? 'ă…' That's **A**nnie **A**pple's sound.

Now let's see how **A**nnie **A**pple likes us to write her letter. Watch, I'm going to start just here, by

her leaf, and go *all* the way round **A**nnie **A**pple, *up* to the top and *down* again. That bit at the bottom stops her from rolling away when she's in a word.

Shall I do that again? I'm going *round* **A**nnie **A**pple, *up* to the top and *down* again. And while I do it, let's all say her special sound, 'ă…, ă…, ă…'.

Can you see all the **a**pple trees? There are lots of **a**pples on the **a**pple trees, but I can see something crawling up the trunk of the **a**pple tree, right down in this corner. Can you see it? Does anybody know what it is? It's a tiny little creepy crawly thing and the word for it starts with **A**nnie **A**pple's sound, 'ă…'. That's right. It's an **a**nt.

Bouncy Ben

Objective

To teach the letter shapes and sound for **b** and **B**.

What you need

Letterland materials

⭐ *Early Years Big Picture Code Cards*: Bouncy Ben
⭐ *Lower Case Pictogram Copymasters*: **b**
⭐ *Early Years Handwriting Copymasters*: 2 and 28
⭐ *Early Years Workbook 1*: pages 6-7

Other materials

⭐ Washing-up liquid
⭐ Blue paint in a jar
⭐ Straws
⭐ Ingredients for making biscuits or buns
⭐ Bread, butter and blackberry jam
⭐ Blue balloon

Teaching suggestions

Introducing Bouncy Ben

Show the children the picture of Bouncy Ben on page 11 of the *ABC Book* and introduce him using **Session 1** from the *Early Years Cassette* as a guide for what to say. Invite one or more children to find and touch Bouncy Ben's brown face on the *Class Wall Frieze*.

Bouncy Ben's letter shape

After **Session 2**, the following handwriting verse, chanted or sung as on the *Handwriting Songs Cassette*, will help in teaching Bouncy Ben's letter shape:

Brush down Ben's big, long ears.
Go up and round his head so his face appears!

Invite one or more children to finger trace Ben's letter shape on the *ABC Book* or on both sides of the *Early Years Big Picture Code Cards*.

Bouncy Ben's sound

To say Bouncy Ben's sound correctly, tell the children to keep their faces still, with their mouths almost completely closed to keep any tendency to add 'uh' to a minimum. In reading, too much 'uh' sound will make blending difficult, e.g. 'buh-e-d' instead of 'be...d'. Bouncy Ben's song on the *Alphabet Songs Cassette* can be listened to and sung, which will help the children to achieve the correct sound.

Bouncy Ben's words

baby	blue
bad	boat
balance	bounce
ball	bread
bat	breakfast
beautiful	bridge
bed	brown
bee .	bubble
big	bun
bird	bus
birthday	butter
biscuit	butterfly

Early Years Cassette transcript

Session 1: Introducing Bouncy Ben
I can see a **b**lue letter on this page. And I can see somebody looking out of the letter. Can you see two **b**lue eyes looking out of the letter? Yes, those **b**lue eyes **b**elong to a Letterland rabbit called **B**ouncy **B**en.
   Can you see his **b**lue **b**all at the **b**ottom of the page? He **b**ounced that **b**all into the **b**ushes. Shall we put our hand out and pretend we've got a **b**all and **b**ounce it?
   Bounce, **b**ounce, **b**ounce goes the **b**all. That's right. Put your **b**all away now, and give your hand a rest.
   Bouncy **B**en loves playing with a **b**all. He does

Things to do

⭐ **Bouncing** Suggest that all the children bounce like Bouncy Ben with both feet together, while making 'b...' sounds. Then let them try bouncing backwards: much harder! Warn them not to bump into each other!

⭐ **Building bridges** Provide construction toys such as building blocks and ask the children to build bridges with them.

⭐ **Butterflies and birds** Let everyone pretend to be butterflies, birds and bees, flying and buzzing around. Then ask everyone to pretend to land on a flower bud.

⭐ **Butterfly pictures** Help the children to make 'butterfly pictures'. To do this, fold a sheet of paper in half. Add a blob of paint on one half. Fold the paper along the crease, smooth down and open again. Add another colour on the first half, fold and smooth down again. Open up the paper and add eyes and feelers. You may need to help with the finishing touches!

⭐ **Bubble pictures** Mix washing-up liquid and blue paint in a jar. Get the children to blow into the paint with a straw until bubbles overflow. (It is wise to check that the children know the difference between blowing and sucking *before* they start this activity!) Then press a sheet of paper onto paint bubbles at the top of the jar and pull off.

⭐ **Cookery** Help the children to make biscuits or buns. They could also eat bread, butter and blackberry jam.

⭐ **Further practice** For extra practice of the letter shape, use the following materials:
– *Lower Case Pictogram Copymasters*: **b**
– *Early Years Handwriting Copymasters*: 2 and 28.
For consolidation of both letter shape and sound use:
– *Early Years Workbook 1*, pages 6-7.

Things to talk about

⭐ **Breakfast** Talk about what the children like to eat for breakfast. What do they think Bouncy Ben would have for breakfast? For instance, you could ask, 'Would he have bread/bacon/baked beans/?' ('Yes.') or 'Would he have cornflakes/eggs/sausages?' ('No.')

⭐ **Balloons** Blow up a big blue balloon and talk about it getting bigger. This can lead on to looking for other words beginning with Bouncy Ben's sound.

Explaining the capital B shape

Bouncy Ben's head is still in the same position in his capital letter shape. The only difference now is that he is balancing his 'best blue ball' between his 'big brown ears'. Explain that Bouncy Ben does this whenever he starts an important word. Let the children take turns at being Bouncy Ben by balancing a balloon on their heads between upraised arms, as in the capital **B**.

---

something special with his **b**ig **b**lue **b**all as well. Sometimes he **b**alances his **b**lue **b**all on top of his head.

Session 2: Bouncy Ben's shape and sound
Let's have a look at **B**ouncy **B**en's **b**lue letter on this page again. Shall we draw it?

I'm going to start at the top of **B**ouncy **B**en's **b**ig **b**rown ear, go *down* his ear, and then I'm going to go **b**ack up *over* his face...and I stop just under his chin.

And while I do it this time, I'm going to say **B**ouncy **B**en's special sound. You listen. **B**ouncy **B**en says '**b**..., **b**..., **b**...'. It's a very *short* little sound. Can you say his short little sound with me? '**B**..., **b**..., **b**...'. Yes, **B**ouncy **B**en says, '**b**...'.

I can see something yellow right at the top of the page. It uses its yellow wings to fly. Do you know what it's called? That's right. It's a **b**utterfly, a **b**eautiful **b**utterfly.

Wait a minute. That word **butterfly** starts with **B**ouncy **B**en's sound, doesn't it! '**B**..., **b**...' **b**utterfly. That's the sound **B**en always makes in words!

And can you see something else that flies in the sky? It has a sting. What's it called? A **b**ee! That's right. It's a **b**uzzy **b**ee.

Who can remember how we draw **B**ouncy **B**en again? Where do we start? Right at the tip of his **b**ig long ears. We go *right* down his ear, then up *around* his face so he is ready to say '**b**..., **b**..., **b**...' for **B**ouncy **B**en.

Clever Cat

Objective

To teach the letter shapes and sound for **c** and **C**.

What you need

Letterland materials

☆ *Early Years Big Picture Code Cards*: Clever Cat
☆ *Lower Case Pictogram Copymasters*: **c**
☆ *Early Years Handwriting Copymasters*: 3 and 29
☆ *Early Years Workbook 1*: pages 8-9
☆ *An Alphabet of Rhymes Book*

Other materials

☆ Pictures of cats
☆ Paper plates
☆ Elastic or tape
☆ Modelling dough
☆ Various coins
☆ Biscuits or cup cakes
☆ Icing sugar
☆ Small sweets

Teaching suggestions

Introducing Clever Cat

Show the children the picture of Clever Cat on page 13 of the *ABC Book* and introduce her using **Session 1** from the *Early Years Cassette* as a guide for what to say. Invite one or more children to find and touch Clever Cat on the *Class Wall Frieze*.

Clever Cat's letter shape

After **Session 2**, the following handwriting verse, chanted or sung as on the *Handwriting Songs Cassette*, will help in teaching Clever Cat's letter shape:

> Curve round Clever Cat's face to begin.
> Then gently tickle her under her chin.

Invite one or more children to finger trace Clever Cat's letter shape on the *ABC Book* or on both sides of the *Early Years Big Picture Code Cards*.

Clever Cat's sound

Clever Cat's sound is an *unvoiced* sound. Make sure that the children practise it in a whisper. It is very important, when it comes to blending sounds, that no child says 'cuh'. Take care especially when singing Clever Cat's song from the *Alphabet Songs Cassette* (see page 72). Stop singing to *whisper* the 'c…' sound.

Clever Cat's words

cake	clothes
can	cold
candles	colour
cap	come
car	cook
castle	count
cat	cross
clean	cuddle
clever	cup
climb	custard
clock	cut

Early Years Cassette transcript

Session 1: Introducing Clever Cat

Let's look at this page. Can you see that **c**at? Have you got a **c**at? Isn't this **c**at a *lovely* **c**at! She has a red letter on her head. That's because she's a *Letterland* **c**at.

Look, she has just settled down to have a picnic in Letterland. Look at all the food she's brought with her. There are **c**ream **c**akes, **c**ucumber sandwiches, and lots of other good things to eat.

She even remembered to bring along her favourite **c**ushion. **C**lever **C**at thinks of everything. That's why people call her **C**lever **C**at.

Can you see some white things in the sky? What are they? That's right. They're **c**louds in the sky. Sometimes when there are *lots* of **c**louds in

Things to do

☆ **Cat collages** Make cat collages by asking the children to draw cats or use cat pictures cut out from cards, calendars and magazines. Mount and display them.

☆ **Paper plate face** Help the children to draw and colour in Clever Cat's face on the back of a paper plate. Then add ears, whiskers, etc., perhaps with scraps of card, paper or fur fabric and string. These could be made into masks by cutting holes to see through and adding elastic or tape ties.

☆ **Cut-outs** Let the children use modelling dough to cut out cat shapes or to make pretend cakes.

☆ **Coin collection** Keep a coin collection going. Each time a child brings in an interesting new coin, you can take a few moments to revise Clever Cat's sound.

☆ **Cookery** The children can make Clever Cat's face on plain biscuits or cup cakes using icing and small sweets.

☆ **Further practice** For extra practice of the letter shape, use the following materials:
– *Lower Case Pictogram Copymasters*: c
– *Early Years Handwriting Copymasters*: 3 and 29.
For consolidation of both letter shape and sound use:
– *Early Years Workbook 1*, pages 8-9.

Things to talk about

☆ **Clever Cat's sound** Talk about what sound cats usually make and then explain that Clever Cat never miaows, but says 'c..., c...' instead. She is the *only* cat that does this.

☆ **Cats** Find out if any of the children have a cat at home. Talk about the things that cats like to eat and drink, such as fish, milk or cream. Explain that because she is a Letterland cat, Clever Cat only eats food that begins with her sound and help the children to think what she would like, e.g. cream cakes, crisps, cucumbers, carrots, cauliflower, etc.

☆ **Caterpillars** Bring in some caterpillars (and leaves) in a suitable clear container. Talk about their colours and movements and explain how they turn into butterflies or moths.

☆ **Rhyme** If available, read the poem 'Clever Cat's Cuddles' from the *Alphabet of Rhymes Book* to the children and try learning the lines together.

Explaining the capital C shape

Explain to the children that whenever Clever Cat starts important words such as names, she takes a deep breath and gets bigger.

---

the sky, what **c**omes out of the **c**louds? Yes. The rain **c**omes.

Look at the picture. Do you think it's going to rain today? No, the sky is blue. **C**lever **C**at has chosen a lovely day for a picnic. Isn't she a **c**lever **c**at!

Session 2: Clever Cat's shape and sound
Can anyone tell us the name of the lovely **c**at here in this picture? Yes, **C**lever **C**at. What's she doing here? Yes, she's having a picnic. Where does **C**lever **C**at live? In Letterland!

Clever **C**at is a very *special* **c**at because she is a *Letterland* **c**at. I've got a **c**at and my **c**at says 'Miaow.' But this **c**at is far too **c**lever to say 'Miaow'. **C**lever **C**at is *so* **c**lever that she makes a special sound instead, like this, '**c**..., **c**..., **c**...'. Can you make that sound with me? Just whisper it, '**c**..., **c**..., **c**...', that's right. Can you hear her little '**c**...' sound

two times as you say her name? Listen, **C**...lever **C**...at?

Let's stroke her, shall we? She likes us to stroke her in a very special way, around her letter. We start by her ear, we go *over* to the other ear, go *round* her face, and we stop under her chin. That's it. Shall we do it again? Let's make her special sound, '**c**..., **c**..., **c**...' as we go round.

Let's see what else we can find in our picture that begins with **C**lever **C**at's sound.

What are those white things up in the sky? **C**louds, yes!

And what is **C**lever **C**at going to eat on her picnic? **C**ream **c**akes! Most **c**ats we know would never eat **c**ream **c**akes. But **C**lever **C**at does. Why? Because she's a *Letterland* **c**at. So she likes to eat anything that begins with her sound. **C**ream **c**akes and **c**ucumber sandwiches for our **C**lever **C**at.

Dippy Duck

Objective

To teach the letter shapes and sound for **d** and **D**.

What you need

Letterland materials

☆ *Early Years Big Picture Code Cards*: Dippy Duck
☆ *Lower Case Pictogram Copymasters*: **d**
☆ *Early Years Handwriting Copymasters*: 4 and 30
☆ *Early Years Workbook 1*: pages 10-11
☆ *An Alphabet of Rhymes Book*

Other materials

☆ Egg boxes or yellow tissue paper
☆ Yellow felt or buttons
☆ Modelling dough
☆ Duck-shaped cutters (if available)
☆ 6 shoe boxes
☆ Dice
☆ Pictures of ducks
☆ Paper 'dinner' plates and dishes

Teaching suggestions

Introducing Dippy Duck

Show the children the picture of Dippy Duck on page 15 of the *ABC Book* and introduce her using **Session 1** from the *Early Years Cassette* as a guide for what to say. Invite one or more children to find and touch Dippy Duck and her Duck Door on the *Class Wall Frieze*.

Dippy Duck's letter shape

After **Session 2**, the following handwriting verse, chanted or sung as on the *Handwriting Songs Cassette*, will help in teaching Dippy Duck's letter shape:

Draw Dippy Duck's back. Go round her tum.
Go up to her head. Then down you come!

Invite one or more children to finger trace Dippy Duck's letter shape on the *ABC Book* or on both sides of the *Early Years Big Picture Code Cards*. Learning the difference between **b** and **d** takes time. The key to correct **d**-shapes are the starting point (Dippy Duck's back) and the discovery that Dippy Duck can be found in the child's right (writing) hand. To see her letter, they just lift their index finger briefly. Left-handers simply copy their free hand!

Dippy Duck's sound

It is very difficult to avoid adding an unwanted 'uh' sound when making Dippy Duck's letter sound. Try to ensure that the children say 'd...' through closed teeth. This way they will manage to keep the 'uh' to a minimum. Dippy Duck's song on the *Alphabet Songs Cassette* provides useful practice in her 'd...' sound.

Dippy Duck's words

Daddy	dish	down
daffodil	doctor	draw
daisy	dog	dress
dance	doll	drink
day	donkey	drum
dinner	door	duck

Early Years Cassette transcript

Session 1: Introducing Dippy Duck

Let's look at this page. What can we see? Yes, there's a yellow **d**uck on this page. Have *you* ever seen a **d**uck swimming on the water?

Look at the **d**uck's feet; they are webbed feet. Webbed feet help **d**ucks to swim and **d**ive **d**own in the water. **D**ucks **d**ip their beaks into the water to **d**rink.

This is our Letterland **d**uck. Her name is **D**ippy **D**uck. She's called **D**ippy **D**uck because she **d**ips her beak into the water to **d**rink and to search for food in the **d**uck pond.

Things to do

⭐ **Duck heads** Make paper duck heads for the children to wear on their right index fingers. Hold them in place with sticky tape.

⭐ **Dippy Duck dance** Let the children waddle about like Dippy Duck, making 'd…' sounds at the same time.

⭐ **Daffodil or daisy pictures** Make daffodil or daisy pictures with the children by cutting out petal shapes to make a flower. For a daffodil, you can use part of an egg box painted yellow for the trumpet, or use tissue paper. Use a circle of yellow felt or a button for the daisy's centre.

⭐ **Dough ducks** Let the children use modelling dough to make dough ducks. Use duck-shaped cutters, if available.

⭐ **Dice game** Remove the lids of six shoe boxes and number them one to six. Line them up on the floor. The children can take turns to throw a dice and then try to throw a ball into the box with the same number on it.

⭐ **Duck den** Turn a corner of the room into a duck den for the week. Add pictures of ducks on the wall, and dinner plates and dishes for serving 'Dippy Duck's dinner'. If possible, make a D-shaped duck door for the children to waddle through into the den, when they pretend to be ducks. Make it low enough so that they have to 'duck down' to go in.

⭐ **Further practice** For extra practice of the letter shape, use the following materials:
– *Lower Case Pictogram Copymasters*: **d**
– *Early Years Handwriting Copymasters*: 4 and 30.
For consolidation of both letter shape and sound use:
– *Early Years Workbook 1*, pages 10-11.

Things to talk about

⭐ **Ducks** Talk about ducks and how they hatch from eggs like chickens. Tell the children that little ducklings are covered with down (very soft, fluffy feathers) and know how to swim right away.

⭐ **Rhyme** If available, sing or read the poem 'Dippy Duck's Song' from the *Alphabet of Rhymes Book* to the children and try learning the lines together.

⭐ **Dippy Duck's words** Help the children to think of words beginning with Dippy Duck's sound, using the box on page 26 for suggestions.

⭐ **Ugly Duckling** Tell the story of 'The Ugly Duckling'.

⭐ **Ducks' song** Teach the song 'Five little ducks went swimming one day'.

Explaining the capital D shape

To help the children to remember the capital D shape, tell them that the funny shaped door with Dippy Duck's head poking out is Dippy Duck's duck door. When they see it at the beginning of a word, they should think of Dippy Duck saying 'd...' just inside her door.

Dippy **D**uck can **d**ive in the **d**uck pond too. Let's say our Letterland **d**uck's name again. Her name is **D**ippy **D**uck.

Session 2: Dippy Duck's shape and sound

Who can remember the name of our **d**uck? Yes, it's **D**ippy **D**uck.

Dippy **D**uck is a special **d**uck because she *never* quacks. She makes a very quiet sound, listen. **D**ippy **D**uck says 'd…, d…, d…'.

She says 'd…' when she is **d**iving. She says 'd…' when she **d**ips her beak into her **d**uck pond to search for food.

Can you say her 'd…' sound with me while I **d**raw round her letter? I'll start to **d**raw over **D**ippy **D**uck's back, I'll go *under* her body, *up* to her head and I then stroke her feathers *down*. **D**id you say 'd…' while I **d**rew **D**ippy **D**uck's letter?

Let's **d**o it again. Start to **d**raw over **D**ippy **D**uck's back, *under* her body, *up* to her head and then stroke her feathers *down* again.

Look, can you see the **d**oor on her house? It's **D**ippy **D**uck's **d**oor. When she goes in there, there's a **d**elicious **d**inner of **d**uckweed and **d**andelions waiting for **D**ippy **D**uck.

Eddy Elephant

Objectives

To teach the letter shapes for **e** and **E** and the short vowel sound 'ĕ...', and to introduce the long vowel sound 'ē...'.

What you need

Letterland materials

☆ *Early Years Big Picture Code Cards*: Eddy Elephant and Mr E
☆ *Lower Case Pictogram Copymasters*: **e**
☆ *Early Years Handwriting Copymasters*: 5 and 31
☆ *Early Years Workbook 1*: pages 12-13

Other materials

☆ Large egg-shaped pieces of paper or card
☆ 3 egg boxes
☆ 12 balls: 6 each of 2 colours
☆ Egg shells
☆ Cotton wool
☆ Cress seed

Teaching suggestions

Introducing Eddy Elephant

Show the children the picture of Eddy Elephant on page 17 of the *ABC Book* and introduce him using **Session 1** from the *Early Years Cassette* as a guide for what to say. Invite one or more children to find and touch Eddy Elephant's face and trunk on the *Class Wall Frieze*.

Eddy Elephant's letter shape

After **Session 2**, the following handwriting verse, chanted or sung as on the *Handwriting Songs Cassette*, will help in teaching Eddy Elephant's letter shape:

Ed has a headband. Draw it and then stroke round his head and his trunk to the end.

Invite one or more children to finger trace Eddy Elephant's letter shape on the *ABC Book* or on both sides of the *Early Years Big Picture Code Cards*.

Eddy Elephant's sound

Tell the children that if they forget Eddy Elephant's sound, they just need to *start* saying his name and the right sound will come straight out of their mouths.

Eddy's song on the *Alphabet Songs Cassette* will also help the children to achieve the correct sound.

Eddy Elephant's words

egg	engine
elbow	enjoy
elephant	enter
eleven	envelope
empty	every
end	exit

Early Years Cassette transcript

Session 1: Introducing Eddy Elephant
What a lot of **e**ggs I can see. Oh dear. I can see a cracked **e**gg. Can *you* see a cracked **e**gg? It's falling over somebody's head. Whose head is the cracked **e**gg falling over? It's an **e**lephant. That's right. This **e**lephant is **E**ddy **E**lephant. Can you see how he wears his lovely red letter on his head? That's because he's a *Letterland* **e**lephant!

Is **E**ddy **E**lephant **e**njoying himself? Do you **e**njoy playing with **e**ggs? How many **e**ggs can you see? Shall we try counting them? Miss out the cracked one. One, two, three, four, five, six.

Wait a minute, I can see two more by his leg, can you? Shall we count those as well? Let's start again. One, two, three, four, five, six, seven, eight. Can you see *another* one on the plate? Eight and

Things to do

⭐ **Egg patterns** Provide the children with egg-shaped pieces of paper or card for them to decorate with patterns. Start a pattern at the top for them and ask them to try to make more rows that look the same. ∿∿∿∿ ℓℓℓℓ ⋔⋔

⭐ **Egg box game** To play the egg box maths game, you need three empty egg boxes, six balls of one colour and six more of another. (If necessary, you can make these with screwed-up pieces of paper.) Get the children to see how many different ways they can fill the boxes, such as 2 red + 4 blue, or 3 red + 3 blue.

⭐ **Egg heads** Help the children to make 'egg heads'. Fill clean, empty egg shells with cotton wool. Using a felt pen, let the children *gently* draw faces on the shells and place them in egg cups. Dampen the cotton wool for them to sprinkle on cress seed and leave to let the 'hair' grow.

⭐ **Further practice** For extra practice of the letter shape, use the following materials:
– *Lower Case Pictogram Copymasters*: **e**
– *Early Years Handwriting Copymasters*: 5 and 31.
For consolidation of both letter shape and sound use:
– *Early Years Workbook 1*, pages 12-13.

Things to talk about

⭐ **Elephants** Talk about elephants and ask if anyone has seen one at the zoo. Ask them if they know why elephants need a long bendy trunk and where they live.

⭐ **Action rhyme** Teach the children the action rhyme 'An elephant goes likes this and that'.

⭐ **Excellent** Talk about the meaning of the word **excellent** and use it as your main word of praise during your 'Eddy Elephant week'.

⭐ **Eddy's objects** Look around the environment with the children for words beginning with Eddy Elephant's letter.

Explaining the capital E shape

Eddy Elephant is very proud of his 'elephant on end' trick. He sits down and points everything – his trunk and all his feet – in the Reading Direction whenever he starts an important word.

Introducing Mr E, the Easy Magic Man

Show the children the picture of Mr E, the Easy Magic Man, on either the *Class Wall Frieze* or on the *Early Years Big Picture Code Cards*. Explain that Mr E looks after Eddy Elephant and has taught him his 'elephant on end' trick. At special times Mr E appears instead of Eddy Elephant and says his name, 'ē...' as in **easy**.

Mr E's words

Easter
easy
eat
even

---

one more makes nine. *And* there's one more in the box. Nine and one more in the box makes ten. If we count the cracked one we have eleven **e**ggs!

There's **E**ddy **E**lephant playing with his **e**ggs. Do you like **e**ggs? Yes, I do. I *love* these special **e**ggs. Which one do you like best? The blue one. Oh, I think I like the yellow one with the red ribbon round it. Can you say **E**ddy **E**lephant's name all together? **E**ddy **E**lephant.

Session 2: Eddy Elephant's shape and sound
Let's have another look at **E**ddy **E**lephant. Shall we make his red letter? Start by his ear, go *across* his forehead, go *over* the top of his head and around, and stop at his mouth just underneath his trunk. Shall we do it again? Start by his ear. Go *across* his forehead first..., and then *over* the top of his head and round, and stop by his mouth. That's **E**ddy **E**lephant.

Shall I tell you a secret about Letterland animals and people? Did you know, you can always find out what sound they make in words by just *starting* to say their names? Let's just start to say '**E**ddy **E**lephant' and see what sound we make. Be ready to put your hand over your mouth so only the first sound comes out. Ready... 'Ĕ...'! Yes, **E**ddy **E**lephant's sound is 'ĕ..., ĕ.... ĕ...' Shall we say it while I stroke his letter, 'ĕ..., ĕ..., ĕ...'.

No wonder **E**ddy **E**lephant likes playing with **e**ggs. Can you think why he's playing with **e**ggs? It's because the word **eggs** starts with **E**ddy **E**lephant's sound. So of course **E**ddy **E**lephant enjoys playing with **e**ggs!

Fireman Fred

Objective

To teach the letter shapes and sound for **f** and **F**.

What you need

Letterland materials

☆ *Early Years Big Picture Code Cards*: Fireman Fred
☆ *Lower Case Pictogram Copymasters*: **f**
☆ *Early Years Handwriting Copymasters*: 6 and 32
☆ *Early Years Workbook 1*: pages 14-15

Other materials

☆ Toy fireman's helmet (if available)
☆ Small magnets
☆ Thin wood dowelling
☆ Toy fire engine or picture of one
☆ Shaving foam or hair-styling mousse

Teaching suggestions

Introducing Fireman Fred

Show the children the picture of Fireman Fred on page 19 of the *ABC Book* and introduce him using **Session 1** from the *Early Years Cassette* as a guide for what to say. Invite one or more children to find and touch Fireman Fred on the *Class Wall Frieze*.

Fireman Fred's letter shape

After **Session 2**, the following handwriting verse, chanted or sung as on the *Handwriting Songs Cassette*, will help in teaching Fireman Fred's letter shape:

First draw Fred's helmet.
Then go down his clothes.
Give him some arms
so he can hold his hose.

Invite one or more children to finger trace Fireman Fred's letter shape on the *ABC Book* or on both sides of the *Early Years Big Picture Code Cards*.

Fireman Fred's sound

'Fff...' is an *unvoiced* sound. Tell the children always to whisper it to avoid saying 'f-uh'. Fireman Fred's song on the *Alphabet Songs Cassette* will help in achieving the correct sound.

Fireman Fred's words

face	fix
fall	flag
farm	flame
fast	flower
favourite	fly
feel	fork
feet	four
fence	fox
fetch	friend
field	frog
fill	from
fireworks	fruit
fish	fun
five	funny

Early Years Cassette transcript

Session 1: Introducing Fireman Fred
Now we're going to meet **F**ireman **F**red. **F**ireman **F**red's a *very* busy man. What do you think he does? Quite right, he puts out fires. Can you see that little bit of fire? Can you see the flames? He's got a big hosepipe that comes all the way from his fire engine. And do you know, **F**ireman **F**red doesn't just use water. He uses **f**oam to put out his fires. Look, some of the **f**oam is **f**alling on him. And there's even **f**oam **f**alling out of the picture!

Why do you think **F**ireman **F**red wears a helmet? I think it's to protect his head when he's near a fire, don't you?

Why do you think he wears boots on his **f**eet? Yes, I think it's to stop his **f**eet from getting wet in

Things to do

☆ **Being firefighters** Let everyone mime being firefighters putting out a big fire.

☆ **Counting fingers** Show how to count five fingers on each hand.

☆ **Counting Fred's buttons** Look at the pictures of Fireman Fred together and ask the children to count the buttons on Fireman Fred's coat.

☆ **Flame pictures** Help the children to make flame or fire pictures using red, yellow and orange finger paints and five fingers.

☆ **Follow my leader** Play Fireman Fred's favourite game of 'Follow my leader'. Choose one child to be the leader and let him or her wear a fireman's helmet, if available.

☆ **Building fire engines** Let the children build fire engines with building bricks.

☆ **Fishing game** Cut out cardboard fish in different colours and sizes and add paper fasteners as eyes or paper clips as mouths. Use small magnets attached to strings and thin wooden dowelling sticks as rods. The children can take it in turns to catch the fish, and then to count the number caught, or look at the colours or sizes of fish caught.

☆ **Further practice** For extra practice of the letter shape, use the following materials:
– *Lower Case Pictogram Copymasters*: f
– *Early Years Handwriting Copymasters*: 6 and 32.
For consolidation of both letter shape and sound use:
– *Early Years Workbook 1*, pages 14-15.

Things to talk about

☆ **Fire engines** Talk about fire engines with the children, asking what they are for, why we need them and what they carry. Use a toy fire engine or a picture to help. Can the children tell you why fire engines make a loud noise and flash blue lights?

☆ **Fred's foam** Bring some shaving foam or hair-styling mousse and squirt a small blob into each child's hand. Use it to explain how Fireman Fred's foam acts like a blanket to put out a fire.

☆ **Fireworks** Discuss fireworks with the children and why we like them. Warn them not to touch fireworks. Tell them that Fireman Fred always puts safety first and likes to make sure that they know never to play with fire or fireworks.

☆ **Favourite foods** Talk about the children's favourite foods. Let them suggest Fireman Fred's favourites, such as fish fingers, fresh fruit and fudge.

☆ **Faces** Using a picture of Fireman Fred, talk about faces and let the children name the different features.

Explaining the capital F shape

Get the children to compare the small and capital **F** on the *Class Wall Frieze*. Let them tell you how the capital letter is the same and how it is different from Fireman Fred's small letter shape.

---

the **f**oam. Can you remember our **f**ireman's name? It's **F**ireman **F**red. Can you say it with me? **F**ireman **F**red.

Look! There's a little brown **f**rog in this corner. He looks **f**rightened, doesn't he! **F**ireman **F**red runs **f**ast so the **f**rog has to jump **f**ast to get out of his way...and to get out of the **f**oam! Can anyone see another **f**rog by the **f**lowers?

Session 2: Fireman Fred's shape and sound

Do you remember our **f**irefighter's name? Yes, it's **F**ireman **F**red. Let's look how we make **F**ireman **F**red's letter.

We start *right* at the top of his helmet and go *all* the way down, and then we go across his arms. Shall we try again? You go *right* down from his

helmet, *all* the way down and then we go *across* his arms. Where do we start writing **F**ireman **F**red's letter? That's right. Right at the top of his helmet.

Can you remember how he puts out the **f**lames? With **fff**oam! And can you hear **F**ireman **F**red's sound? '**Fff**..., **fff**...'.

Shall we say '**F**ireman **F**red' together? Let's call him. '**F**ireman **F**red, **F**ireman **F**red!' Listen to his '**fff**...' sound as we call his name, '**F**ireman **F**red.'

Can you see some other things that start with his '**fff**...' sound? Yes, we can see the **f**lames and the **f**oam. Let's ask him to put the fire out. '**F**ireman **F**red, please put the fire out with your **f**oam.'

Golden Girl

Objective

To teach the letter shapes and sound for **g** and **G**.

What you need

Letterland materials

- ☆ *Early Years Big Picture Code Cards*: Golden Girl
- ☆ *Lower Case Pictogram Copymasters*: **g**
- ☆ *Early Years Handwriting Copymasters*: 7 and 33
- ☆ *Early Years Workbook 2*: pages 2-3

Other materials

- ☆ Items for a miniature garden
- ☆ Pictures of flowers
- ☆ Coloured paper
- ☆ Icing sugar
- ☆ Green food colouring
- ☆ Green grapes
- ☆ Assorted gloves, including gardening gloves

Teaching suggestions

Introducing Golden Girl

Show the children the picture of Golden Girl on page 21 of the *ABC Book* and introduce her using **Session 1** from the *Early Years Cassette* as a guide for what to say. Invite one or more children to find and touch Golden Girl on the *Class Wall Frieze*. Ask them to touch her green clothes and her glasses (which she wears for reading). Talk briefly about her go-cart letter, if asked.

Golden Girl's letter shape

After **Session 2**, the following handwriting verse, chanted or sung as on the *Handwriting Songs Cassette*, will help in teaching Golden Girl's shape:

Go round Golden Girl's head.
Go down her golden hair.
Then curve to make her swing
so she can sit there.

Invite one or more children to finger trace Golden Girl's letter shape on the *ABC Book* or on both sides of the *Early Years Big Picture Code Cards*, and also to find the go-cart on the frieze.

Golden Girl's sound

Ask the children to *start* saying Golden Girl's name and they will find her sound in the back of their throats. (If you have a George or Gemma in your group, explain that Golden Girl sometimes gives her best friend 'Gentle Ginger' a turn in her go-cart and her swing.) Golden Girl's song on the *Alphabet Songs Cassette* will help in achieving the correct sound.

Golden Girl's words

garden	golden
get	goldfish
giggle	good
girl	grandfather
give	grandmother
glasses	grapes
glue	grass
go	green
goat	grow

Early Years Cassette transcript

Session 1: Introducing Golden Girl

Who's swinging on this swing? That's right, it's a **g**irl...a **g**irl with long **g**olden hair. Do you think she likes swinging? Yes, I think she does, because she's smiling while she swings. We call her **G**olden **G**irl because of her **g**olden hair. Can you say her name with me? **G**olden **G**irl!

I *do* like **G**olden **G**irl's **g**arden. Look at that **g**reen **g**rass.

Oh! She'd better move her foot. There's a **g**rey animal **g**obbling **g**rapes by her foot. Can you see what animal that is? Yes, it's a **g**oat and **g**oats **g**obble up anything. They will **g**obble **G**olden **G**irl's shoe if she doesn't move it out of the way.

Things to do

⭐ **Pretend glasses** Let the children pretend to put some glasses on and then take them off again. Ask them where they could put them when they are not using them (on their heads, just like Golden Girl).

⭐ **Miniature garden** Help the children to grow a miniature garden, either using real garden materials, such as grass seed, moss, cress, flowers, etc. or by making modelling dough flowers.

⭐ **Things in the garden** Go out into a garden together, if possible, and look for items beginning with Golden Girl's sound, such as a gate, grass, grasshoppers, grey and green things, ground, gravel, grit and greenhouse.

⭐ **Gorgeous garden picture** Give help in drawing a 'gorgeous garden' picture by filling a sheet of paper with flowers from edge to edge. Alternatively, the children could make one, using pictures of flowers cut out from magazines or seed catalogues. They can then give it as a gift to their grandparents.

⭐ **Cookery** Help the children to add green icing to biscuits, or let them sample some green grapes.

⭐ **Further practice** For extra practice of the letter shape, use the following materials:
– *Lower Case Pictogram Copymasters*: **g**
– *Early Years Handwriting Copymasters*: 7 and 33.
For consolidation of both letter shape and sound use:
– *Early Years Workbook 2*, pages 2-3.

Things to talk about

⭐ **Favourite colours** Talk about the children's favourite colours. Show them some green, yellow, silver and gold paper or other items. Which colours might Golden Girl like best? (The ones beginning with her sound: green and gold.)

⭐ **Wearing glasses** Ask if anyone wears or knows someone else who wears glasses, and talk about how glasses can help us.

⭐ **Gloves** Show the children different kinds of gloves and mittens. Look at how many places each kind has for fingers. Talk about how gardening gloves differ from other gloves.

⭐ **Giving gifts** Golden Girl loves giving grapes from her garden to all her friends. Discuss giving gifts.

Explaining the capital G shape

 When Golden Girl is needed to start an important word, she gets out of her swing and gets into her go-cart. Whereas on her swing she is not looking in the Reading Direction, when she is in her go-cart, she has to look where she is going, so that she does not bump into the other Letterland characters. She always uses her go-cart letter to start her name, Golden Girl. She makes her usual 'g...' sound as she goes.

Let's tell her, '**G**olden **G**irl, there's a **g**oat **g**obbling **g**rapes by your foot!'
Can you call her again? '**G**olden **G**irl.'

Session 2: Golden Girl's shape and sound

Can you remember *this* **g**irl's name? Yes, it's **G**olden **G**irl. She has **g**olden hair. While she swings we hear the sound, '**g**..., **g**..., **g**...' for **G**olden **G**irl.

This swing is an unusual one. Look, this piece goes *round* her head and then there's a gently curving piece for her to sit on.

I'm going to draw her swing while we all say her '**g**...' sound. Start at the top, go *round* her head, *up* to the rope, *down* and curve *round* to make a swing. Let's do it again while we say her '**g**...' sound. Go round her head, up to the rope, down and curve

round to make her **g**arden swing.

Can you see her **g**arden **g**ate? What **g**rey animal was that **g**obbling **g**reen **g**rapes in her **g**arden? Yes, her **g**oat. Why should **G**olden **G**irl keep her **g**arden **g**ate shut? Yes, otherwise her **g**oat might **g**o out of the **g**ate and **g**et lost.

I can see a **g**reenhouse with plants **g**rowing in it. I'm **g**lad that **G**olden **G**irl's swing is not too near the **g**reenhouse, because **g**reenhouses are make of **g**...? Yes, **g**reenhouses are made of **g**lass.

Sometimes **G**olden **G**irl **g**ets out of her swing and **g**ets into her **g**o-cart. Look at her **g**oing fast on her **g**o-cart. She *always* uses her **g**o-cart letter to start her name, **G**olden **G**irl.

Hairy Hat Man

Objective

To teach the letter shapes and sound for **h** and **H**.

What you need

Letterland materials

- ☆ *Early Years Big Picture Code Cards*: Hairy Hat Man
- ☆ *Lower Case Pictogram Copymasters*: **h**
- ☆ *Early Years Handwriting Copymasters*: 8 and 34
- ☆ *Early Years Workbook 2*: pages 4-5

Other materials

- ☆ One or more boxes
- ☆ Green tissue paper
- ☆ As many hats as possible

Teaching suggestions

Introducing Hairy Hat Man

Show the children the picture of the Hairy Hat Man on page 23 of the *ABC Book* and introduce him using **Session 1** from the *Early Years Cassette* as a guide for what to say. Invite one or more children to hop over to the *Class Wall Frieze* and touch Hairy Hat Man's head and his heels. Explain the capital H shape if asked (see opposite).

Hairy Hat Man's letter shape

After **Session 2**, the following handwriting verse, chanted or sung as on the *Handwriting Songs Cassette*, will help in teaching Hairy Hat Man's letter shape:

> Hurry from the Hat Man's head
> down to his heel on the ground.
> Go up and bend his knee over,
> so he'll hop while he makes his sound.

Invite one or more children to finger trace Hairy Hat Man's letter shape on the *ABC Book* or on both sides of the *Early Years Big Picture Code Cards*.

Hairy Hat Man's sound

This sound is really a little sigh, or panting sound, to be whispered. Make sure nobody adds voice, turning 'hhh…' into 'huh'. That hurts the Hat Man's ears! The Hairy Hat Man's song on the *Alphabet Songs Cassette* will help in achieving the correct sound.

Hairy Hat Man's words

ham	hill
hand	his
happy	holly
hat	home
hear	honey
hedge	horrible
hedgehog	horse
helicopter	hot
helpful	house
hen	how
her	huge
here	hungry

Early Years Cassette transcript

Session 1: Introducing the Hairy Hat Man

I can see Harry, the Hairy Hat Man. Do you know why I call him the Hairy Hat Man? Because he *always* wears that green hairy hat on his head. Can you see it right here?

It *is* a hairy hat isn't it! He has a hairy beard as well, hasn't he? And he's holding his hand up. I think he's waving 'hello' to us! Let's all wave 'hello' to him. Put your hand up, ready? All together, 'Hello, Hairy Hat Man!'

Oh dear. I forgot! The Hairy Hat Man hates noise, so we had better do that again much more quietly. Let's call out in a whisper: 'Hello, Hairy Hat Man.' Ah, lovely and quiet. That's *exactly* how the Hat Man likes it.

I can see the Hairy Hat Man's house on the hill.

Things to do

⭐ **Hand play** The children can put their hands on their head, heel, hip, other hand, hair and heart, in any order that you say. End with everyone holding hands.

⭐ **Hairy Hat Man picture** Make a huge picture of the Hairy Hat Man together and then display it. Get the children to make hand-prints on small pieces of paper, cut them out, label and display them around it. Add pictures of other objects starting with the Hat Man's sound.

⭐ **Hunt the hat** Hide a picture of the Hat Man's hat and choose a child to look for it. Say 'Warmer, warmer' as the child gets nearer to the hiding place, and 'Hot!' when he or she is beside it.

⭐ **Hairy Hat Man's house** Help the children to make the Hat Man's house, using a box for the base and folded card for the roof. Cover the roof with glued on pieces of screwed up green tissue paper.

⭐ **Hopping** Go outside and let the children take turns hopping towards the other children, who can listen to their panting 'hhh…' sounds as they arrive.

⭐ **Further practice** For extra practice of the letter shape, use the following materials:

– *Lower Case Pictogram Copymasters*: **h**
– *Early Years Handwriting Copymasters*: 8 and 34. For consolidation of both letter shape and sound use:
– *Early Years Workbook 2*, pages 4-5.

Things to talk about

⭐ **Hats** Ask the children to bring in all kinds of hats and use those collected in 'Clever Cat's Costume Box', (see **Dressing up** on page 17). Talk about who would wear them, and why.

⭐ **Horrible noise** Ask if any child hates noise and if they know anyone else who also hates noise, perhaps their parents or teacher. Do they think that they are sometimes too noisy? Stress consideration for other people.

⭐ **Houses and homes** Talk about the Hat Man's unusual house using page 23 of the *ABC Book*, and let the children compare it with their own homes. Talk about what homes are made from and look at those of various animals, e.g. a dog kennel, bird cage or nest, fox den, rabbit hutch or burrow, etc.

⭐ **Helping hands** Talk about how our hands help us and then try using just one. Discuss how we can use our hands to help others, such as helping at home by tidying up, etc.

Explaining the capital H shape

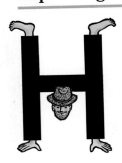

Tell the children that when the Hat Man has a chance to start a name, he is so happy that he does a handstand with his hat on! To write his capital letter, they need to start up at the Hat Man's heel, go from his heel to hand, heel to hand. Then they can draw the line across.

But there's something odd about his **house**. What is that on top of it? It looks more like a **hat** than a roof!

My **house** has a roof on it. Does your **house** have a roof on it? But the **Hat** Man's **house** has a **hat** for a roof! I wonder **how** that **happened**, don't you?

Session 2: Hairy Hat Man's shape and sound

Can you think why our friend here has no shoes on? It's because he **hates** noise.

Too much noise gives him a **horrible headache**, so he doesn't even wear shoes because shoes make too much noise as he **hops** along.

When the **Hairy Hat** Man goes into a word, do you know what sound he makes? You have to whisper it, like this: '**hhh**…' Can you **hear** it at the start of his name? **Hhh**arry the **Hhh**airy **Hhh**at

Man. Did you **hear** that '**hhh**…' sound at the beginning of his name?

Watch while we make **Hairy Hat** Man's letter. We start at his **head** and go *down* his long back, right to his **heel**. Then we go back up *over* his knee and stop at his other **heel**. Let's do it again and whisper his '**hhh**…' sound as we start at his **head** …, go *down* to his **heel**…, go up *over* his knee …and down to his other **heel**. Remember, **Hairy Hat** Man says '**hhh**…'.

What can we see in the sky? It isn't a plane. You're quite right, it's a **helicopter**.

Harry, the **Hairy Hat** Man is **happy** that the **helicopter** is **hurrying** off. **Helicopters** are noisy and what does the **Hairy Hat** Man **hate**? Noise! That's why he **himself** never speaks above a whisper, '**hhh**…'.

Impy Ink

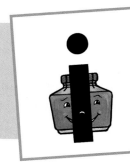

Objectives

To teach the letter shapes for **i** and **I** and the short vowel sound 'ĭ...', and to introduce the long vowel sound 'ī...'.

What you need

Letterland materials

☆ *Early Years Big Picture Code Cards*: Impy Ink and Mr I
☆ *Lower Case Pictogram Copymasters*: **i**
☆ *Early Years Handwriting Copymasters*: 9 and 35
☆ *Early Years Workbook 2*: pages 6-7

Other materials

☆ Pictures of insects
☆ Bottle of ink
☆ Ball-point pen
☆ Rubber stamps
☆ Ink pad
☆ Newspapers

Teaching suggestions

Introducing Impy Ink

Before introducing the short 'ĭ...' sound, it is good idea to revise the short 'ă...' and 'ĕ...' sounds first. Then show the children the picture of Impy Ink on page 25 of the *ABC Book* and introduce him using **Session 1** from the *Early Years Cassette* as a guide for what to say. Invite one or more children to find and touch Impy Ink and the ink pen on the *Class Wall Frieze*. Talk briefly about Mr I, the Ice Cream Man, too, if asked (see opposite).

Impy Ink's letter shape

After **Session 2**, the following handwriting verse, chanted or sung as on the *Handwriting Songs Cassette*, will help in teaching Impy Ink's letter shape:

Inside the ink bottle draw a line.
Add an inky dot. That's fine!

Invite one or more children to finger trace Impy Ink's letter shape on the *ABC Book* or on both sides of the *Early Years Big Picture Code Cards*.

Impy Ink's sound

Tell the children just to *start* saying 'Impy Ink' to find his little 'ĭ...' sound. See who can hear his sound in their name, either at the start or inside it. Impy Ink's song on the *Alphabet Songs Cassette* will help in pronouncing his sound correctly.

Impy Ink's words

if	insect
ill	inside
important	interesting
in	into
infants	invitation
ink	itch

Early Years Cassette transcript

Session 1: Introducing Impy Ink

I can see a blue bottle on this page. Do you know what's in this bottle? It's something called ink. You can pour ink. You can pour it out of the bottle. If we didn't keep ink in a bottle it would make a *terrible* mess because it spills very easily.

In Letterland, all the school children use special ink pens to write with. Can you see a special pen in the corner? I have one like that, too. I dip it into the ink, and I fill the pen up with ink and then I can write with it. But when I write with ink, the ink is wet, so I have to be very careful and wait for it to dry.

Can you see the ink pen and the bottle of ink?

Things to do

☆ **Insect pictures** Collect pictures of insects. Help to make insect pictures with different colour paint blobs. Add three legs on either side.

☆ **Ink** Bring in a real bottle of ink to show the children and show them the ink stem in a plastic ball-point pen. Let them use an ink pad to press rubber stamp pictures on to paper. They could also crumple up newspapers and look at their hands afterwards. Explain that it is ink that makes them dirty.

☆ **Further practice** For extra practice of the letter shape, use the following materials:
– *Lower Case Pictogram Copymasters*: i
– *Early Years Handwriting Copymasters*: 9 and 35.
For consolidation of both letter shape and sound use:
– *Early Years Workbook 2*, pages 6-7.

Things to talk about

☆ **Introductions** Make a game of introducing each other. Ask each child to say one or two things about another child, such as, 'His/Her name is…, he/she lives near…, has a baby brother, likes…, his/her favourite food (game, song) is…', etc. Extend the game by asking the children to introduce themselves - or even you!

☆ **Going into things** Together think of as many things as possible that we can go *into*, such as a house, kitchen, bedroom, car, tent, sea, rain, sun, wind, trouble, dark, light, field, garden, town, shops, library, etc.

☆ **Important things** Talk about things that are important, such as safety, kindness, brushing teeth (cleanliness), and also things that are important in the children's personal lives, such as grandparents coming, etc.

☆ **Interesting** Use the word **interesting** as often as possible during your 'Impy Ink week'.

Explaining the capital I shape

Explain that when Impy Ink takes a deep breath, his letter gets so tall and thin that you can't see his ink spot any more. His letter looks like his ink pen instead.

Introducing Mr I, the Ice Cream Man

Show the children the picture of Mr I, the Ice Cream Man, on either the *Class Wall Frieze* or on the *Early Years Big Picture Code Cards*. Explain that Mr I is a very important person in Letterland because he sells ink and ice cream, and that at times he also says his name 'ī…' in words.

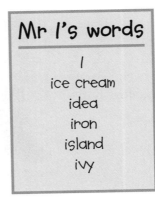

Mr I's words

I
ice cream
idea
iron
island
ivy

There's a smiling face on that bottle of ink. That face belongs to Impy Ink. Can you say his name for me? Impy Ink. That's right. Impy Ink lives in the Letterland school.

To fill the ink pen, we take the top off Impy Ink and put the ink pen into his ink and fill it up.

Let's pretend to dip the ink pen into Impy Ink's bottle while we say his name: Impy Ink.

Session 2: Impy Ink's shape and sound
Can you remember who this is on this page? Yes, it's Impy Ink. Impy Ink makes an 'i…' sound. Let's say it while we pretend to put the ink pen into Impy Ink. 'I…, i…, i…'.

Look at Impy Ink's letter. To write his letter I go *straight* down his bottle and then I put a dot on top.

Can you do it with me? Start at the top, go *straight* down and put his dot on top. Then we say, 'i…' for Impy Ink. Can you say it for me? Impy Ink says 'i…, i…'.

Now let's say it together while we draw his letter. Start at the top, go *down* his letter, put a dot on top and say 'i…, i…'.

I can see two little creatures who should not be near the ink. Can you see the tiny little creatures at the bottom of the page? They are insects.

Insects have six legs. If they put their legs in the wet ink, they will make ink marks all across the page. I think we ought to move those insects away from Impy Ink, don't you! Otherwise there will be ink marks everywhere.

Jumping Jim

Objective

To teach the letter shapes and sound for **j** and **J**.

What you need

Letterland materials

☆ *Early Years Big Picture Code Cards*: Jumping Jim
☆ *Lower Case Pictogram Copymasters*: **j**
☆ *Early Years Handwriting Copymasters*: 10 and 36
☆ *Early Years Workbook 2*: pages 8-9

Other materials

☆ Green paper
☆ Large box
☆ Coffee jar lids
☆ Jam, jelly or fruit juice
☆ Sponge or soft balls for juggling
☆ Stiff wire
☆ Old greeting cards
☆ Envelopes
☆ Jack-in-a-box (if available)

Jumping Jim's sound

To say Jumping Jim's sound correctly, ask the children to just start saying his name and they will find his sound pushing itself out of their mouths. Jim's song on the *Alphabet Songs Cassette* will also help them to pronounce Jim's sound correctly.

Jumping Jim's words

jacket	journey
jam	joy
January	jug
jar	juggle
jaw	juice
jelly	July
jigsaw	jump
job	jumper
jog	June
joke	jungle
jolly	just

Teaching suggestions

Introducing Jumping Jim

Show the children the picture of Jumping Jim on page 27 of the *ABC Book* and introduce him using **Session 1** from the *Early Years Cassette* as a guide for what to say. Invite one or more children to jump up and touch Jumping Jim on the *Class Wall Frieze*.

Jumping Jim's letter shape

After **Session 2**, the following handwriting verse, chanted or sung as on the *Handwriting Songs Cassette*, will help in teaching Jumping Jim's letter shape:

> Just draw down Jim, bending his knees.
> Then add the one ball which everyone sees.

Invite one or more children to finger trace Jumping Jim's letter shape on the *ABC Book* or on both sides of the *Early Years Big Picture Code Cards*.

Early Years Cassette transcript

Session 1: Introducing Jumping Jim

Before I get out my book, we're all going to stand up. Now we're going to make three **j**umps. Ready. We're going to **j**ump now...**j**ump...and another one...**j**ump... and another one...**j**ump. Oh, well done! That's *three* big **j**umps. Now if we sit down *very*, *very* carefully and rest our **j**umping feet, I've got a picture to show you. Are you ready?

Look at my picture. And what's *this* boy doing? Yes, he's **j**umping as well. What a big **j**ump he's making. He's **j**umping all the way through Letterland! I'll tell you his name. His name is **J**umping **J**im. Can you say it for me? **J**umping **J**im. That's right. **J**umping **J**im **j**umps through Letterland, **j**ust like we've been **j**umping.

Jumping **J**im does something else that's very,

Things to do

☆ **Jumping Jim's jungle** Let the children tear assorted green paper into leaves. Join the leaves into leaf chains and hang them from the ceiling for a jungle effect.

☆ **Junk box** Label a 'Junk Box' and encourage everyone to collect oddments, for use this week and in the future.

☆ **Jim's jeep** Ask the children to draw, paint or make a junk model jeep for Jumping Jim. Stick coffee jar lids onto the jeep for wheels.

☆ **Jim's jet** Help to make model jet planes, using junk from the Junk Box (see above).

☆ **Food tasting** Try some jam, jelly or juice tasting and let the children decide on their favourites.

☆ **Juggling** Let the children try some juggling, possibly outside, either with sponge balls or small, soft balls. You could also thread sponge balls onto a circle of stiff wire to use for pretending to be Jumping Jim juggling.

☆ **Jumps** Set up jumps in the playground for jumping over, or items for jumping off.

☆ **Jigsaws** Help the children to make their own jigsaw puzzles. Let them draw a picture, or use old greeting cards, then cut them into four, five or six pieces. They can then try putting the jigsaw pieces back together again. They may like to take their jigsaw home in an envelope to reassemble there.

☆ **Further practice** For extra practice of the letter shape, use the following materials:
– *Lower Case Pictogram Copymasters*: **j**
– *Early Years Handwriting Copymasters*: 10 and 36.
For consolidation of both letter shape and sound use:
– *Early Years Workbook 2*, pages 8-9.

Things to talk about

☆ **Months of the year** Ask everyone to listen carefully as you recite the months of the year and get them to raise their hands when they hear a month starting with Jumping Jim's sound (January, June and July).

☆ **Jack-in-a-box** Find out if a child has a Jack-in-the-box that they can bring in to show everybody, or provide one yourself.

☆ **Journeys** Talk about long and short journeys with the children, perhaps to the shops, to visit relatives, etc. Ask what Jumping Jim would need to take with him on a long journey (jeans, jumpers, etc.), or where he might go to (Japan, Jerusalem, etc.).

Explaining the capital J shape

In Letterland, whenever Jumping Jim can start an important word, he is so pleased, that he does a big jump, and his head disappears in the clouds. We can then no longer see his ball.

very clever. Can you see what he has in his hand? Yes, he has a ball. But Jumping Jim doesn't throw just one ball. He can sometimes throw one, two, three balls all together. Does anybody know what that's called? It's called juggling. And Jumping Jim can juggle. He can throw three balls up in the air and catch another ball at the same time!

I find it hard to throw *one* ball up and catch it. I can't throw three balls up and catch them one, two, three. Jumping Jim can. Let's say his name as he juggles those balls. Jumping Jim. That's right.

Session 2: Jumping Jim's shape and sound
Can you remember who this is? Yes, it's Jumping Jim. He can jump and juggle. Do you know what sound Jumping Jim makes when he jumps into words? Just start to say his name,'J…' Yes, Jumping Jim says, 'j…' at the beginning of his name and in words like jump and juggle. Let's

say his sound while we draw him.

Can you start just under his hand where he's holding the ball. We go *all* the way down his leg and *round* to his jumping shoes. Shall we try it again? Start at his hand where he's holding the ball, go *all* the way down his leg and *round* to his jumping shoes. And don't forget to give him a spot for a little jumping juggling ball. Let's do it again and this time we will say 'j…' for Jumping Jim.

Sometimes he jumps so high, you can't see his ball. It's hidden by the clouds. Just look. There's something else in those clouds. Can you see a plane in the clouds?

I wonder what sort of plane it is. If it belongs to Jumping Jim, it will start with his special 'j…' sound. That's right. It's a jet plane in the sky behind Jumping Jim.

Kicking King

Objective

To teach the letter shapes and sound for **k** and **K**.

What you need

Letterland materials

☆ *Early Years Big Picture Code Cards*: Kicking King
☆ *Lower Case Pictogram Copymasters*: **k**
☆ *Early Years Handwriting Copymasters*: 11 and 36
☆ *Early Years Workbook 2*: pages 10-11

Other materials

☆ Coloured paper or card
☆ Gummed paper
☆ Tin foil
☆ Newspaper
☆ Tray or wide box
☆ Kaleidoscope
☆ Old magazines or catalogues
☆ Kiwi fruit or tin of fruit including kiwi slices
☆ Bag of sugar, or something weighing a kilo
☆ Bathroom scales (if available)

Teaching suggestions

Introducing Kicking King

Show the children the picture of Kicking King on page 29 of the *ABC Book* and introduce him using **Session 1** from the *Early Years Cassette* as a guide for what to say. Invite one or more children to find and touch Kicking King on the *Class Wall Frieze*. They could also touch his arm and his kicking foot.

Kicking King's letter shape

After **Session 2**, the following handwriting verse, chanted or sung as on the *Handwriting Songs Cassette*, will help in teaching Kicking King's letter shape:

Kicking King's body is a straight stick.
Add his arm, then his leg, so he can kick!

Invite one or more children to finger trace Kicking King's letter shape on the *ABC Book* or on both sides of the *Early Years Big Picture Code Cards*.

Kicking King's sound

Explain that Kicking King and Clever Cat are very pleased that they both make exactly the same sound in words. The king is too busy looking after the kingdom to appear in many words, so he is glad that Clever Cat can do the job in most words. Kicking King's song on the *Alphabet Songs Cassette* will help in teaching the correct sound.

Kicking King's words	
kaleidoscope	kid
kangaroo	kilo
keep	kind
kennel	king
ketchup	kiss
kettle	kitchen
key	kite
kick	kitten

Early Years Cassette transcript

Session 1: Introducing Kicking King

I can see a **k**ing on this page. How do I know that he is a **k**ing? Yes, he's wearing a crown on his head, but this is an unusual **k**ing. Just look at his feet! What's he doing? He's **k**icking a ball.

Our **k**ing loves playing football. He loves **k**icking that ball. That's why we call him **K**icking **K**ing. But do you know, he's a very **k**ind **k**ing as well. And because he is a very **k**ind **k**ing, he only ever **k**icks footballs. I'm pleased about that.

There's an animal on this page. I think he wants to join in the football game as well, because

Things to do

⭐ **King's crowns** Hand out strips of paper with a zig-zag edge for the children to decorate as Kicking King's crowns, perhaps with pieces of coloured gummed paper or foil. Then staple them together for the children to wear.

⭐ **Kicking balls** Show how to make paper balls out of screwed up newspaper. Take turns trying to kick the balls into a tray or wide box. See how many balls are in the box and practise counting 0, 1, 2, 3, etc.

⭐ **Kite pictures** Draw some kite shapes on the top half of pieces of paper. The children can complete the pictures by drawing Kicking King in below, then adding lines from the kites to his hand.

⭐ **Kaleidoscope** Take turns viewing through a kaleidoscope. Explain that Kicking King loves looking through one, too.

⭐ **Kitchen collage** Help to make a kitchen collage, using pictures cut out of magazines or catalogues.

⭐ **Kiwi fruit** Bring in a fresh kiwi fruit for the children to share, or tinned fruit which includes kiwi slices.

⭐ **Further practice** For extra practice of the letter shape, use the following materials:
– *Lower Case Pictogram Copymasters*: **k**
– *Early Years Handwriting Copymasters*: 11 and 36.
For consolidation of both letter shape and sound use:
– *Early Years Workbook 2*, pages 10-11.

Things to talk about

⭐ **Kittens** In Letterland, Kicking King keeps his kittens in his kitchen. Ask if anyone has a kitten and where they keep it.

⭐ **Kindness** Talk about kindness and explain that the King is a kind king who is kind to people and to animals, especially his kittens, pet kangaroo, and koala bear. Ask who is kind to the children, and how they can be kind, for instance, to each other, to brothers and sisters and to pets.

⭐ **Kangaroo, koala and kookaburra** Talk about all these creatures from Australia and show pictures of them, if available. You could also sing the song 'Kookaburra sits in the old gum tree'.

⭐ **Kilo** Bring in some objects to show how heavy a kilo is, such as a bag of sugar. Ask the children to see if they can find out at home how many kilos they weigh. Alternatively, bring in some scales and weigh each child.

⭐ **Names** Find out if any of the children have, or know someone with, a first or surname beginning with Kicking King's letter, such as Kate, Katie, Katherine, Kevin, Khaleda, etc.

Explaining the capital K shape

Tell the children that when Kicking King starts an important word, he takes a deep breath. His arm and kicking leg then get longer so he will look more important in that word.

---

he is very good at **k**icking too. Do you know what animal he is? He's a very unusual animal. He has huge, long back legs and very short front legs. He's a **k**angaroo.

Kangaroos like **k**icking. I think this **k**angaroo is going to help our **K**icking **K**ing play football. 'Don't kick **K**icking **K**ing, **k**angaroo, will you!'

Session 2: Kicking King's shape and sound
I think you've remembered who this is. Yes, it's **K**icking **K**ing. Can you say **K**icking **K**ing's sound for me. It's '**k**...' for kick and '**k**...' for king. Let's say it together. **K**icking **K**ing says, '**k**..., **k**...'. And when we draw him, we start *right* by his neck. We go

down to his foot and then we *start* by his hand, go *in* to his waist and *out* to his **k**icking foot.

Shall we do that again? Start by his head, go *right* down to his foot. Start by his hand, go to his waist and out to his **k**icking foot. Let's say his sound again, '**k**..., **k**...' for **K**icking **K**ing.

When **K**icking **K**ing isn't playing football, he likes to do something else outside. Look in this corner. Can you see something the same colour as **K**icking **K**ing's football? It's a **k**ite. Sometimes **K**icking **K**ing takes his **k**ite outside. Why do you think he likes to fly **k**ites? Yes, because **kite** starts with **K**icking **K**ing's '**k**...' sound.

Lucy Lamp Lady

Objective

To teach the letter shapes and sound for **l** and **L**.

What you need

Letterland materials

☆ *Early Years Big Picture Code Cards*:
   Lucy Lamp Lady
☆ *Lower Case Pictogram Copymasters*: **l**
☆ *Early Years Handwriting Copymasters*: 12 and 37
☆ *Early Years Workbook 2*: pages 12-13

Other materials

☆ Envelopes
☆ Old cotton reels
☆ White cotton wool
☆ Pipe cleaners
☆ Lettuce
☆ Lemon
☆ Lemonade
☆ Lemons
☆ Leeks
☆ Lentils
☆ Labels (luggage ones, if available)
☆ Various leaves
☆ Torch
☆ Bicycle lamp
☆ Other types of lights (if available)

Teaching suggestions

Introducing Lucy Lamp Lady

Show the children the picture of Lucy Lamp Lady on page 31 of the *ABC Book* and introduce her using **Session 1** from the *Early Years Cassette* as a guide for what to say. Invite one or more children to find and touch Lucy Lamp Lady on the *Class Wall Frieze*. If asked, talk briefly about her capital letter shape, too (see opposite).

Lucy Lamp Lady's letter shape

After **Session 2**, the following handwriting verse, chanted or sung as on the *Handwriting Songs Cassette*, will help in teaching Lucy Lamp Lady's letter shape:

Lamp Lady looks like one long line.
Go straight from head to foot
and she's ready to shine!

Invite a child to finger trace down Lucy's long straight letter on the *ABC Book* or on both sides of the *Early Years Big Picture Code Cards*.

Lucy Lamp Lady's sound

The best way to avoid adding an unwanted 'uh' sound to 'lll…' is to keep the tip of your tongue touching the roof of your mouth. This will make blending sounds much easier: not 'lluh-eg' but 'llleg' for **leg**. Lucy Lamp Lady's song on the *Alphabet Songs Cassette* will help in achieving the correct sound.

Lucy Lamp Lady's words

ladder	lighthouse
lamb	like
lamp	little
large	live
laugh	long
leaf	look
left	lost
leg	lots
lemon	lovely
letter	lunch

Early Years Cassette transcript

Session 1: Introducing Lucy Lamp Lady
Here's a very long, tall lady. Look at that hat she's wearing on her head. Yes, it's like a lamp shade. There is light coming from her hat.

This lady is called **Lucy** and she's called the **Lamp Lady**. Can you say her name with me? **Lucy Lamp Lady**.

Can you see those little animals looking at her? They are little lambs. They're looking at **Lucy Lamp Lady**.

Look, in the distance there is a lighthouse. The lighthouse is by the sea and the lighthouse has a

Things to do

☆ **Leaping up** Play 'Lucy Lamp Lady says "Leap up!"' Start with everyone lying down as low down as they can. They must then all leap up and try to be long and thin like Lucy.

☆ **Lucy's lighthouse** Help the children to paint a large picture of Lucy's lighthouse (you may need to help them with the outline) and display it prominently on the wall. The children can make a long ladder with construction kit pieces and lean it against the lighthouse picture.

☆ **Letters** Provide paper and envelopes for the children to make pretend letters to Mummy, Daddy, Granny or even Lucy, and display the letters to her around the lighthouse picture (see above).

☆ **Little lambs** Make some little lambs together with cotton reels covered in cotton wool and pipe cleaner legs.

☆ **Lunch** For lunch, eat or drink as many things as possible beginning with Lucy's sound, such as lettuce and lemonade. The children could also have a look at lemons, leeks and lentils.

☆ **Labels** Prepare labels for various objects in the classroom beginning with **l** (use luggage labels if available) and get the children to label correctly the light switch, library books, etc.

☆ **Further practice** For extra practice of the letter shape, use the following materials:
– *Lower Case Pictogram Copymasters*: 1
– *Early Years Handwriting Copymasters*: 12 and 37.
For consolidation of both letter shape and sound use:
– *Early Years Workbook 2*, pages 12-13.

Things to talk about

☆ **Length** Talk about length to the children and ask how long their left hand is. Let each child in turn (so that everyone is watching) measure something with their hand, and then ask how many hands long it is. See who has the longest hand in the room.

☆ **Leaf display** Make a collection of leaves. Talk about their different shapes and colours and compare the fronts and backs. Use them to make a leaf display around a brown paper tree.

☆ **Lights** Bring in a torch, a bicycle lamp and any other lights. Talk about why we need traffic lights, street lights, lighthouses, etc.

☆ **Ladders** Talk about the people who might use a ladder, such as decorators, (painting a house), builders, window cleaners, firemen, etc.

☆ **Ladybirds** Talk about ladybirds and what they look like. Stress that they eat tiny flies in the garden.

Explaining the capital L shape

Explain that whenever Lamp Lady starts important words, she takes a deep breath and gets bigger. In her case, however, her legs also grow longer, so long in fact, that she has to sit down with her legs on the line.

If you can, take a photograph of all the girls sitting in a line miming Lucy in her capital letter position. Display the photograph by the lighthouse.

---

big light shining from it.

The lighthouse helps the ships at sea find their way in the dark. When they are a long way out at sea, they can see the light from the lighthouse.

Lucy Lamp Lady is nearly as tall as the lighthouse. Look at her long body. Can you say her name with me? Lucy Lamp Lady.

Session 2: Lucy Lamp Lady's shape and sound

Do you remember the name of this tall lady? Yes, her name is Lucy Lamp Lady. Let's say her name together: Lucy Lamp Lady. She makes a 'lll...' sound. Listen, Lucy Lamp Lady says 'lll...'. Can

you say that with me? Lucy Lamp Lady says 'lll..., lll...'.

I can see one, two, three little animals looking at her. What are they called? Lambs. That's right! Listen. Their name starts with Lucy Lamp Lady's sound, 'lll...', lambs, and, 'lll...', Lucy Lamp Lady.

Let's see if we can make Lucy Lamp Lady's letter. It's so easy! It starts *right* at the top under her chin and just goes *straight* down to her feet. It's just one long line. You try with me. Start at her chin and go straight down to her feet. We can even say her sound while we do it, 'lll...'. Lucy Lamp Lady says, 'lll...'.

Munching Mike

Objective

To teach the letter shapes and sound for **m** and **M**.

What you need

Letterland materials

☆ *Early Years Big Picture Code Cards*: Munching Mike
☆ *Lower Case Pictogram Copymasters*: **m**
☆ *Early Years Handwriting Copymasters*: 13 and 38
☆ *Early Years Workbook 2*: pages 14-15

Other materials

☆ Tin foil
☆ Milk bottle tops
☆ Milk bottles
☆ Metal spoons
☆ Cereal boxes
☆ Egg cartons
☆ Material or buttons for eyes
☆ Button mushrooms
☆ Marshmallows
☆ Magnets
☆ Magnetic objects

Teaching suggestions

Introducing Munching Mike

Show the children the picture of Munching Mike on page 33 of the *ABC Book* and introduce him using **Session 1** from the *Early Years Cassette* as a guide for what to say. Invite one or more children to find and touch Munching Mike on the *Class Wall Frieze*. Ask them to touch his metal head, metal tail, his three metal wheels and his metal mouth.

Munching Mike's letter shape

After **Session 2**, the following handwriting verse, chanted or sung as on the *Handwriting Songs Cassette*, will help in teaching Munching Mike's letter shape:

Make Munching Mike's back leg first,
then his second leg, and third,
so he can go munch-munching in a word.

Invite one or more children to finger trace Munching Mike's letter shape on the *ABC Book* or on both sides of the *Early Years Big Picture Code Cards*.

Munching Mike's sound

To make Munching Mike's sound, ask everyone simply to shut their mouths and hum, and they will be making his sound. Further practice can be found by listening to and singing Mike's song on the *Alphabet Songs Cassette*.

Munching Mike's words

magnet	mix
man	monkey
mat	monster
me	morning
meet	most
melon	mug
metal	Mummy
milk	mushroom
miss	my

Early Years Cassette transcript

Session 1: Introducing Munching Mike

There's a **monster** on this page. He's a *lovely* **monster**. He's a **monster** that is **made** out of **metal**. If you look, there's something very special about him. He has *three* legs. Let's count them, one, two three. How unusual! **Most** creatures have *four* legs or just *two* legs. But not *three* legs like our **monster**.

Our **monster** is called **Munching Mike** because he loves to **munch** when he's eating. And you will never believe what **Munching Mike** the **monster** likes to eat. **Metal!**

Do you like to eat **metal**? No, I don't. But

Things to do

⭐ **Munching Mike model** Help to make a model of Munching Mike or a large picture of the metal monster with foil or milk bottle tops. Make sure he has three legs, not four.

⭐ **Milk bottle music** Make music using milk bottles. Fill them with water to different levels and get the children to tap metal spoons against them to make different notes. Explain that this is Munching Mike's favourite kind of music.

⭐ **Monster masks** Help the children to make monster masks. Cut out the backs of cereal boxes and get them to decorate the front and sides. Use paint, egg box parts, etc. and material or buttons for eyes and ears.

⭐ **Mushroom pictures** Cut in half some firm, button mushrooms. Get the children to press them on to a sponge full of paint and print with them to create 'marvellous mushroom pictures that will make Munching Mike's mouth water'.

⭐ **Marshmallows** Give out some marshmallows to munch as a treat and then say 'Mmm..., delicious!' together.

⭐ **Monsters** Let everyone pretend to be monsters. Groups of three children can make one metal monster together.

⭐ **Further practice** For extra practice of the letter shape, use the following materials:

– *Lower Case Pictogram Copymasters*: **m**
– *Early Years Handwriting Copymasters*: 13 and 38.
For consolidation of both letter shape and sound use:
– *Early Years Workbook 2*, pages 14-15.

Things to talk about

⭐ **Menu** Make up a menu for Munching Mike together, not necessarily just food. He eats mops, mats, mugs, metal, magnets, even mushy mud, as well as meat, melons, etc.

⭐ **Magnets** Talk about magnets and let the children see what happens when they put one near paperclips or other magnetic objects.

⭐ **Mistakes** Talk about mistakes. Say that Mike often makes them and gets into muddles, but explain that luckily mistakes often help us to learn.

Explaining the capital M shape

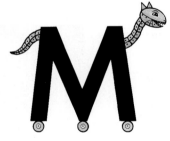

Tell the children that Munching Mike may look big, but he's really only a little monster (too little to start important words), so his Mum does the job for him. Ask them how their mums (or dads) help them.

Munching Mike likes to eat metal. He's eaten a bit of the motorbike.

If we look at the bottom of the page, we can see some other things that Munching Mike likes to eat. He has eaten a map. He's eaten part of a mushroom. And I think if we're not careful, he will eat that magnet as well. What a monster! Munching Mike is a metal-eating monster.

Will you be safe when you are with Munching Mike? Oh, yes! Munching Mike won't want to eat you. You are not made of metal.

Session 2: Munching Mike's shape and sound
I'm sure you'll remember our monster's name. Yes, it's Munching Mike. Look, Munching Mike has three legs.

When we make Munching Mike's letter, we start by his tail! Are you ready? Let's *start* by his tail, go *down* one leg, back up, *over* to the next leg, back and *over* to his front leg.

Shall we do it again? Let's start by his tail, go *down* his leg, back up *over* to the next leg and down, back *over* to the front leg and down, and stop. Remember he has one, two, three legs!

Munching Mike makes the 'mmm...' sound. Can you say it with me? Let's say it while we write his letter. Where do we start? By his tail, that's right. Ready? '**Mmm**..., **mmm**...,' and again, '**mmm**..., **mmm**...' for **M**unching **M**ike.

Naughty Nick

Objective

To teach the letter shapes and sound for **n** and **N**.

What you need

Letterland materials

☆ *Early Years Big Picture Code Cards*: Naughty Nick
☆ *Lower Case Pictogram Copymasters*: **n**
☆ *Early Years Handwriting Copymasters*: 14 and 39
☆ *Early Years Workbook 3*: pages 2-3

Other materials

☆ Newspaper
☆ Sticky tape
☆ Coloured beads or plastic straws
☆ String or laces
☆ Shredded wheat
☆ Chocolate
☆ Paper cake cases
☆ Mini chocolate eggs (if available)
☆ Assorted nuts, including conkers or acorns (if available)
☆ Flower seeds

Teaching suggestions

Introducing Naughty Nick

Show the children the picture of Naughty Nick on page 35 of the *ABC Book* and introduce him using **Session 1** from the *Early Years Cassette* as a guide for what to say. Invite one or more children to find and touch Naughty Nick on the *Class Wall Frieze*. Ask the children to also touch Nick's nose, his nails in **n** and his capital letter shape **N**.

Naughty Nick's letter shape

After **Session 2**, the following handwriting verse, chanted or sung as on the *Handwriting Songs Cassette*, will help in teaching Naughty Nick's letter shape:

'Now bang my nail,' Naughty Nick said.
'Go up and over around my head.'

Invite one or more children to finger trace Naughty Nick's letter shape on the *ABC Book* or on both sides of the *Early Years Big Picture Code Cards*.

Naughty Nick's sound

Ask the children to press a hand on their nose while they make Nick's 'nnn...' sound. They will then feel it through the nose as well as hearing it. If they forget his sound, they can just *start* to say Nick's name. Nick's song on the *Alphabet Songs Cassette* will also help in achieving the correct sound.

Naughty Nick's words

nails	nice
name	night
nap	nine
near	no
neck	noise
need	nose
needle	not
nest	now
net	number
never	nurse
new	nursery
next	nuts

Early Years Cassette transcript

Session 1: Introducing Naughty Nick
I can see a boy on this page. His **n**ame is **N**ick. **N**ow **N**ick is a **n**ice boy, but sometimes he is very **n**aughty, which is **n**ot so **n**ice. In fact, **N**ick has annoyed enough people in Letterland for them to decide to give him a **n**ickname. Do you know what his **n**ickname is? It's **N**aughty **N**ick.

Let's see what **N**aughty **N**ick has in his hands. Yes, he has a hammer in one hand. But what has he got in this hand? A **n**ail. That's right. He's **n**ailing a big **n**ail into a piece of wood. I wonder if he has asked if he can do it. I expect **n**ot!

Do you know what else **N**aughty **N**ick likes to do? He likes to eat **n**uts off his **n**eighbour's tree, without asking. Can you see the little brown **n**uts

Things to do

✰ **Nick's nails** The children can make big, harmless nails out of twisted or rolled newspaper and sticky tape. They can make rows of **N**'s with them or use them for counting games.

✰ **Necklaces** Let the children make necklaces to wear or take home to their mothers. Get them to count out nine beads or nine pieces of chopped up coloured plastic straws, and thread them onto string or laces.

✰ **Cookery** Make some edible nests. To do this, the children mix shredded wheat into melted chocolate and spoon it into paper cake cases. Add mini chocolate eggs, if available, or cut out little birds from paper folded in half.

✰ **Further practice** For extra practice of the letter shape, use the following materials:
– *Lower Case Pictogram Copymasters*: **n**
– *Early Years Handwriting Copymasters*: 14 and 39. For consolidation of both letter shape and sound use:
– *Early Years Workbook 3*, pages 2-3.

Things to talk about

✰ **Naughty or nice?** Discuss naughty and nice behaviour together. Ask if any of the children can think of a time when they were naughty, and if they felt happy or sad afterwards. Then ask if it makes other people, and themselves, happy when they are nice. Tell them that Naughty Nick often forgets, but he is slowly learning that being nice is more fun for everyone.

✰ **Nuts** Provide nuts of different kinds, including conkers or acorns, if available, and compare their different sizes and shapes. Compare tree seeds (nuts) with flower seeds, and talk about how one nut can become a big tree that produces hundreds of other nuts. You could then all sing 'I had a little nut tree'.

✰ **What's new?** Ask if anyone has something new or some new news to share. See if they can notice anything new in the room. You could hang a new number from the ceiling every day.

Explaining the capital N shape

Explain to the children that Nick starts important words by using three big nails, which they can see in Naughty Nick's name. Tell them that to write his big letter shape, they need to go down the first nail, back up again, down the sloping nail and up the last nail.

---

on his **n**eighbour's tree?

Have you **n**oticed something else in that **n**eighbour's tree? I can see a **n**est in the **n**ut tree. And over here I see a **n**et. I wonder what **N**ick uses that **n**et for. Perhaps we'll find out later.

Goodbye for **n**ow, **N**aughty **N**ick. Try **n**ot to be too **n**aughty before we see you again.

Session 2: Naughty Nick's shape and sound
Do you remember this boy's name? Yes, it's **N**aughty **N**ick. **N**aughty **N**ick has a friend called **N**aughty **N**icola. She is one of his **n**ext door **n**eighbours. When **N**aughty **N**ick isn't busy playing with **n**ails, he likes to take his **n**et and go fishing for **n**ewts with **N**aughty **N**icola.

Have you **n**oticed how many **n**uts there are

right **n**ow on that **n**ut tree **n**ext to **N**aughty **N**ick? Later I will leave this book open so you can count the **n**uts and tell me how many you can see.

Now look at **N**aughty **N**ick's letter. Look at the letter with a **n**ail in it. To write **N**ick's letter, we **n**eed to start at the top by the **n**ail and go *down* the **n**ail, and then back round *over* **N**aughty **N**ick's head.

Naughty **N**ick makes the sound at the start of his **n**ame, **Nn**naughty **Nn**nick. Can you say '**nnn**…'? Let's say '**nnn**…' together while we make **N**aughty **N**ick's letter again.

Now you know the '**nnn**…' sound **N**aughty **N**ick makes in words.

Oscar Orange

Objectives

To teach the letter shapes for **o** and **O** and the short vowel sound 'ŏ...', and to introduce the long vowel sound 'ō...'.

What you need

Letterland materials

☆ *Early Years Big Picture Code Cards*: Oscar Orange and Mr O
☆ *Lower Case Pictogram Copymasters*: **o**
☆ *Early Years Handwriting Copymasters*: 15 and 40
☆ *Early Years Workbook 3*: pages 4-7

Other materials

☆ Orange tissue paper
☆ Tray
☆ 6 small objects
☆ Toy typewriter(s) (if available)
☆ Toy telephone(s)
☆ Any 'office' equipment
☆ Pipe cleaners or pairs of tights (4 if dense or 8 if thin)
☆ Needle and thread
☆ Orange sponge paints
☆ Oranges

Teaching suggestions

Introducing Oscar Orange

The vowel sounds are the most important sounds for the children to know well, as they occur so often in words. Build in some revision time for all the short vowels learnt so far: the short 'ă...', 'ĕ...' and 'ĭ...' sounds. Then show the children the picture of Oscar Orange on page 37 of the *ABC Book* and introduce him using **Session 1** from the *Early Years Cassette* as a guide for what to say. Invite one or more children to find and touch Oscar Orange on the *Class Wall Frieze*. Ask them to touch him on his nose and on his mouth. Talk briefly about Mr O, the Old Man, too, if asked (see opposite).

Oscar Orange's letter shape

After **Session 2**, the following handwriting verse, chanted or sung as on the *Handwriting Songs Cassette*, will help in teaching Oscar Orange's letter shape:

> On Oscar Orange start at the top.
> Go all the way round him, and...then stop!

Invite one or more children to finger trace Oscar Orange's letter shape on the *ABC Book* or on both sides of the *Early Years Big Picture Code Cards*.

Oscar Orange's sound

Listen and sing Oscar's song on the *Alphabet Songs Cassette*, which will help the children to achieve the correct short 'ŏ...' sound.

Oscar Orange's words

object	often
October	on
octopus	opposite
odd	or
of	orange
off	ostrich
office	otter

Early Years Cassette transcript

Session 1: Introducing Oscar Orange
I can see something I like on this page. That's right. It is a nice round...**o**range, yes! Do you like **o**ranges? Do you eat **o**ranges?

When you eat an **o**range, does all the juice come out? Oh, yes! It sometimes dribbles down your chin, doesn't it? An **o**range is a round juicy fruit. An **o**range rolls away if you're not careful.

But I've never seen an **o**range with such a smiley face before, have you? This Letterland **o**range has a special name. His name is **O**scar **O**range. Can you say that for me? **O**scar **O**range. That's right. **O**scar **O**range is a big round **o**range.

Things to do

⭐ **Orange week** Have a special 'orange week' and get everyone to bring in orange objects for an orange collection. Make a feature of a large Oscar Orange, made by the children by sticking crushed orange tissue paper onto a circular outline and then adding arms and a face. Encourage the children to wear something orange, if possible.

⭐ **Object game** Play a 'remember the object' game. Place six objects on a tray. While the children close their eyes, put on or take off one object. They look again at the tray and then name the object you put on or took off.

⭐ **Office** Create an office area using toy typewriters, toy telephones, writing pads, etc. The children can pretend to do office work.

⭐ **Oscar's octopus** The children can draw or paint an octopus or make one out of pipe cleaners: this will be good practice for counting to eight. Alternatively, stuff four pairs of dense tights (or eight pairs doubled up) with paper, then tie them together. Use the top of one to make the head and sew it up. Paint the octopus orange using sponge paints and use it for display or play.

⭐ **Further practice** For extra practice of the letter shape, use the following materials:
– *Lower Case Pictogram Copymasters*: o
– *Early Years Handwriting Copymasters*: 15 and 40.
For consolidation of both letter shape and sound use:
– *Early Years Workbook 3*, pages 4-7.

Things to talk about

⭐ **Oranges** Bring in a few oranges to talk about. Ask the children if they know where they come from, why they don't grow easily in our gardens, what they grow on, what colour they are and why they have pips (seeds) inside. Ask if any children like oranges or orange juice.

⭐ **Opposites** Talk about the meaning of the word **opposite**. Discuss opposites such as on and off, day and night, hot and cold, etc.

Explaining the capital O shape

Tell the children that when Oscar Orange is needed to start an important word, he takes a deep breath and gets bigger. Then he gets on with making his 'ŏ...' sound as usual.

Introducing Mr O, the Old Man

Introduce Mr O, the Old Man, using either the *Class Wall Frieze* or the *Early Years Big Picture Code Cards*. Explain that Mr O brings oranges to Letterland from over the ocean by boat. Nobody knows how old he is, but they do know he is old, because of his white beard. At special times Mr O goes into words and says his name, 'ō...', as in **old**.

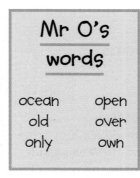

Mr O's words	
ocean	open
old	over
only	own

Is his letter shape round too? Yes, it is! Let's say his name again, **O**scar **O**range.

That's a very **o**dd creature in the sea, as well. It's an **o**ctopus. An **o**ctopus has eight legs. How many **o**ranges is our **o**ctopus holding? Yes, he's holding two **o**ranges. Hello, **o**ctopus! See if you can catch the **o**ranges that drop from **O**scar **O**range's net!

Session 2: Oscar Orange's shape and sound
Here's our **o**range with a smiley face again. Can you remember his name? Yes, he's called **O**scar **O**range. Look at his round shape. His letter shape is round too, isn't it!

When we want to write **O**scar's letter, we start over here by his hand, we go *over* the top of his head, *all* the way round *under* **O**scar **O**range and back up to his hand. Are you ready? Start at his hand. Go *over* the top of his head, all the way round **O**scar **O**range and back up to his hand.

Can you hear the sound at the beginning of **O**scar's name: 'ŏ..., ŏ..., ŏ...'? Did you know when you say his sound, your mouth makes a round shape, like his letter? You look at my mouth and I'll look at your mouth. Shall we say it together? 'Ŏ... ŏ...'. Did my mouth look like a big round letter? Your mouth did, as well! 'Ŏ..., ŏ...' for **O**scar **O**range.

Poor Peter

Objective

To teach the letter shapes and sound for **p** and **P**.

What you need

Letterland materials

☆ *Early Years Big Picture Code Cards*: Poor Peter
☆ *Lower Case Pictogram Copymasters*: **p**
☆ *Early Years Handwriting Copymasters*: 16 and 41
☆ *Early Years Workbook 3*: pages 8-9

Other materials

☆ Pattern-making or mosaic peg boards
☆ Potatoes
☆ Pink and purple paint
☆ Dried pasta (in a variety of shapes)
☆ Prize for 'Pass the parcel'
☆ Paper bags
☆ Any foods beginning with **p**

Teaching suggestions

Introducing Poor Peter

Show the children the picture of Poor Peter on page 39 of the *ABC Book* and introduce him using **Session 1** from the *Early Years Cassette* as a guide for what to say. Invite one or more children to find and touch Poor Peter on the *Class Wall Frieze*. Ask them to point to his droopy ear, his pink nose, his purple collar and his paws.

Poor Peter's letter shape

After **Session 2**, the following handwriting verse, chanted or sung as on the *Handwriting Songs Cassette*, will help in teaching Poor Peter's shape:

> Pat Poor Peter properly.
> First stroke down his ear,
> then up and round his face
> so he won't shed a tear.

Invite one or more children to finger trace Poor Peter's letter shape on the *ABC Book* or on both sides of the *Early Years Big Picture Code Cards*.

Poor Peter's sound

This is one of the sounds which needs to be whispered to avoid adding 'uh'. The sound is simply a puff of air pushed through closed lips. It may help the children to imagine they are panting like a puppy, while making the 'p...' sound. Poor Peter's song on the *Alphabet Songs Cassette* will also help them to achieve the correct sound.

Poor Peter's words

paint	pink
paper	play
parcel	please
park	pond
party	pony
pass	present
paw	pretty
pen	puddle
pencil	pull
pet	puppy
picture	purple
pig	put

Early Years Cassette transcript

Session 1: Introducing Poor Peter

There's a **p**uppy on this **p**age. Oh, he doesn't look at all happy. He looks *very* sad. Do you know why he looks so sad? Let me tell you. He has long droopy ears and this **p**uppy can't make those ears **p**rick up. They always droop down. **P**oor **p**uppy, he would love to have ears that **p**rick up. That's why he's crying. Can you see his tears falling **p**lip, **p**lop into that **p**uddle? We call him **P**oor **P**eter, because we feel sorry for him.

Even the **p**enguins in the **p**ark feel sorry for him. Can you see the **p**enguins in the **p**ark? How many can you see? One..., two.

Things to do

⭐ **Patterns** The children can experiment with making patterns on paper by repeating different lines or shapes, for instance, by drawing round a couple of objects and then repeating the sequence to make a pattern. They could also play with any pattern-making boards or mosaic peg boards.

⭐ **Potato printing** Do some potato printing with the children. Cut potatoes into a variety of shapes, including petal shapes and paw shapes. Make prints using pink and purple paint.

⭐ **Pasta pictures** Provide sheets of coloured paper and get the children to paste dried pasta shapes on to them, perhaps adding paint once they have dried.

⭐ **'Pass the parcel'** Play 'Pass the parcel', Poor Peter's favourite game.

⭐ **Poor Peter puppets** Help the children to make Poor Peter puppets, or puppets of their favourite Letterland characters. Cut out photocopies of the desired characters from the *Lower Case Pictogram Copymasters* or the *Early Years Handwriting Copymasters* and paste them on to paper bags. The children can then colour them in or paint them. Try having a little puppet show with them.

⭐ **People pictures** Ask the children to draw pictures of people. Encourage an eye for detail, such as not forgetting the nose, or hands and feet.

⭐ **Poor Peter's foods** Possibilities for snacks include popcorn, pretzels, peaches, pears or pancakes.

⭐ **Further practice** For extra practice of the letter shape, use the following materials:
– *Lower Case Pictogram Copymasters*: **p**
– *Early Years Handwriting Copymasters*: 16 and 41.
For consolidation of both letter shape and sound use:
– *Early Years Workbook 3*, pages 8-9.

Things to talk about

⭐ **Politeness** Tell the children that Poor Peter always says, '*Please* stroke me properly.' Ask them if they say 'please' often enough, and suggest that they let Poor Peter help them to remember to say it whenever needed, especially this week.

⭐ **Making plans** Talk about making plans. Perhaps the children could help to plan a party and make or wrap up little prizes for party games.

⭐ **Parents** Help everyone to think of ways that they can give some pleasure to their parents.

Explaining the capital P shape

Explain that when Poor Peter has a chance to start an important word, he is so pleased, that he pops up so that everyone can see him better. He hopes his ears will pop up too, but sadly they still droop.

Is this one a **p**enguin? No, it's a different shape and a different colour. This bird is a **p**igeon. I think the **p**igeon and the **p**enguins want to **p**lay with **P**oor **P**eter in the **p**ark, don't you? They **p**robably want to cheer him up.

Come on, **P**oor **P**eter, cheer up. Take your **p**aws out of that **p**uddle and **p**lay in the **p**ark.

Session 2: Poor Peter's shape and sound

Can you remember this **p**uppy's name? Yes, it's **P**oor **P**eter. Do you think if you gently stroke his **p**oor droopy ears you could cheer him up? He loves to have you stroke his ear when you write his letter. Shall I show you how he likes it? We start at the top of his droopy ear, we go *down*, up and *round* his face and finish under his chin. Let's

cheer him up right now, shall we!

Start at the top of his droopy ear, go *down*, up and *round* his face and stop under his chin. Let's make **P**oor **P**eter's sound too. It's a little **p**anting sound, like when a **p**uppy is out of breath, '**p**..., **p**..., **p**...'. You try it, '**p**..., **p**..., **p**...'. while I stroke his ear.

Poor **P**eter will soon feel happy if we always stroke down his droopy ear first. His tears will soon stop. Do you remember the noise his tears made when they fell into the **p**uddle? That's right. Can you say it with me? **P**lip, **p**lop. **P**lip, **p**lop.

Why! Those words, **p**lip, **p**lop start with **P**oor **P**eter's sound, don't they?! '**P**...' for **p**lip and '**p**...' for **p**lop! That's **P**oor **P**eter's sound.

Quarrelsome Queen

Objective

To teach the letter shapes and sound for **q** and **Q**.

What you need

Letterland materials

☆ *Early Years Big Picture Code Cards*: Quarrelsome Queen
☆ *Lower Case Pictogram Copymasters*: **q**
☆ *Early Years Handwriting Copymasters*: 17 and 41
☆ *Early Years Workbook 3*: pages 10-11

Other materials

☆ Card or paper for crowns (gold if available)
☆ Coloured paper (preferably gummed) or tin foil
☆ Paper squares
☆ Old magazines or other patterned paper

Teaching suggestions

Introducing Quarrelsome Queen

Show the children the picture of Quarrelsome Queen on page 41 of the *ABC Book* and introduce her using **Session 1** from the *Early Years Cassette* as a guide for what to say. Invite one or more children to find and touch Quarrelsome Queen on the *Class Wall Frieze*. Ask them to point to her crown and her beautiful long hair.

Quarrelsome Queen's letter shape

After **Session 2**, the following handwriting verse, chanted or sung as on the *Handwriting Songs Cassette*, will help in teaching Quarrelsome Queen's letter shape:

> Quickly go round the Queen's cross face.
> Then comb her beautiful hair into place.

Invite one or more children to finger trace Quarrelsome Queen's letter shape on the *ABC Book* or on both sides of the *Early Years Big Picture Code Cards*.

Quarrelsome Queen's sound

Quarrelsome Queen's sound is really two others put together: 'kw...'. The queen's song on the *Alphabet Songs Cassette* will help in achieving the correct sound.

Quarrelsome Queen's words

quack
quarrelsome
quarter
queen
question
queue
quick
quiet
quill
quilt
quite
quiz

Early Years Cassette transcript

Session 1: Introducing Quarrelsome Queen
Oh, dear. Did you know there's a **q**ueen in Letterland? How do I know she's a **q**ueen? That's right. She always has a crown on her head. But just look at her face. I'd better tell you this **q**uietly. She's a **q**uarrelsome **q**ueen.

Do you ever **q**uarrel? Yes, I **q**uarrel sometimes. When I **q**uarrel, I feel as cross as that **q**ueen looks. **Q**uarrelling makes me feel sad. Does it make you feel sad? Soon after I've **q**uarrelled I have to go back and say, 'I'm sorry.' That makes me feel better again.

When this **q**uarrelsome **q**ueen **q**uarrels, she feels sad afterwards, too. She tells herself she'll

Things to do

⭐ **Queen's crown** Prepare strips of gold or yellow card or paper to make into Quarrelsome Queen's crowns. If neither are available, use white card coloured in by the children. Decorate with gummed coloured paper or tin foil. Then staple each crown to fit the children.

⭐ **Queuing game** Tell the children to make a queue and to move quietly. Direct them to move the queue forwards, or to move the queue to one side. Then move the queue round a chair and move it quickly to the mat or carpet.

⭐ **Queuing picture** On a large piece of paper, draw or paint the Queen on the far right, and then let the children draw or paint pictures of themselves in a queue to see her.

⭐ **Quarters** Help the children to fold square pieces of paper in half twice to make quarters. Ask them to colour each quarter a different colour and then count how many colours they have used.

⭐ **Queen's quilt collage** Make a Queen's quilt collage together by pasting coloured or patterned paper (from magazines, etc.) onto a large sheet of paper. The Queen's face can then be drawn in at the top of it. Don't let the children forget to add her umbrella, too!

⭐ **Further practice** For extra practice of the letter shape, use the following materials:
– *Lower Case Pictogram Copymasters*: **q**
– *Early Years Handwriting Copymasters*: 17 and 41.
For consolidation of both letter shape and sound use:
– *Early Years Workbook 3*, pages 10-11.

Things to talk about

⭐ **Queen's umbrella** The transcript below points out that the Quarrelsome Queen never goes anywhere without her umbrella, because **q** never appears in words without **u**. Two children can act this out in front of the others. One child can be dressed up as the queen, and another one can hold up a real umbrella and follow her around the room. This will also help to avoid confusion between the **p** and **q** letter shapes.

⭐ **Quarrelsome Queen's quarrelling** Invite the children to suggest why Quarrelsome Queen quarrels with some of the Letterland characters. Maybe it is because Naughty Nick makes too much noise banging nails or perhaps Robber Red took her ruby ring?

⭐ **Being quiet** Talk about being quiet. See who can say their name using the quietest voice. Let them take it in turns to try. Then see who can walk with quiet steps and who can stand up and sit down so quietly that we cannot hear them.

⭐ **Being quick** Tell the children that the Queen often says, 'Quick, quick!' See how quickly they can tidy up today.

Explaining the capital Q shape

This very different capital letter shape is the 'Queen's Quiet room'. It has nothing in it except a place for her to sit very quietly.

---

stop, but before she knows it, she's **q**uarrelling again. She's always **q**uarrelling. That's why we call her **Q**uarrelsome **Q**ueen.

And do you know something else that's special about the Letterland **q**ueen? She never goes anywhere without her umbrella. Do you see it there beside her? **Q**uarrelsome **Q**ueen *always* has her umbrella with her when she goes into words.

Session 2: Quarrelsome Queen's shape and sound
If you look at this **q**ueen's face you'll easily remember her name. Yes, it's **Q**uarrelsome **Q**ueen. She's even **q**uarrelling with a squirrel!

Can you remember what **Q**uarrelsome **Q**ueen

takes with her wherever she goes? Yes, she always takes her umbrella with her. **Q**uarrelsome **Q**ueen says 'kw…' for **q**uarrel, 'kw…' for **q**ueen. It's a very **q**uiet sound.

Shall we make her letter? We start off by her crown, we go *all* the way round her face, *up* to her crown and *down* her long hair. Let's try again. We start by her crown, go *round* her face, *up* to her crown and *down* her long hair. And let's make her **q**uiet sound together. 'Kw…, kw…' for **Q**uarrelsome **Q**ueen.

The **Q**ueen has a big round **Q**uiet Room that she goes into after she's been **q**uarrelling. But she even takes her umbrella there. Be **q**uiet, now. We don't want to disturb the **Q**uarrelsome **Q**ueen.

Robber Red

Objective

To teach the letter shapes and sound for **r** and **R**.

What you need

Letterland materials

☆ *Early Years Big Picture Code Cards*: Robber Red
☆ *Lower Case Pictogram Copymasters*: **r**
☆ *Early Years Handwriting Copymasters*: 18 and 42
☆ *Early Years Workbook 3*: pages 12-13

Other materials

☆ Large tray or smooth board
☆ Variety of small objects, some of which must roll
☆ Several shades of red paper

Teaching suggestions

Introducing Robber Red

Show the children the picture of Robber Red on page 43 of the *ABC Book* and introduce him using **Session 1** from the *Early Years Cassette* as a guide for what to say. Invite one or more children to find and touch Robber Red on the *Class Wall Frieze*. Ask them to touch his red cap, red legs and red boots. Talk about the capital **R** pictogram if asked (see opposite).

Robber Red's letter shape

After **Session 2**, the following handwriting verse, chanted or sung as on the *Handwriting Songs Cassette*, will help in teaching Robber Red's letter shape:

Run down Robber Red's body.
Go up to his arm and his hand.
Then watch out for this robber
roaming round Letterland.

Invite one or more children to finger trace Robber Red's letter shape on the *ABC Book* or on both sides of the *Early Years Big Picture Code Cards*.

Robber Red's sound

Children will need to avoid adding an unwanted 'uh' sound by keeping their teeth touching while making Robber Red's growling sound.

They must not move their chins as they 'growl'. Robber Red's song on the *Alphabet Songs Cassette* will help in achieving the correct sound.

Robber Red's words

rabbit	red	roof
race	ride	rope
radio	right	roses
rain	ring	round
rascal	road	rubber
rat	robber	rules
read	robot	run
ready	rock	ruler
really	roll	run

Early Years Cassette transcript

Session 1: Introducing Robber Red
Now here's **R**obber **R**ed. **R**obber **R**ed is a **r**eal **r**ascal. He takes things that don't belong to him. We don't like that, do we!

Can you see what he has in his hand? Yes! He has a **r**ing. He has a **r**ed **r**ing in his hand.

Ah! Look at the things in his sack. He has taken some **r**oller skates. He has taken somebody's **r**adio. And I think I can see a big piece of **r**ope as well.

Robber **R**ed **r**uns very quickly. Why do you think he **r**uns? Yes! So that people can't catch him up and see all the things that he has taken.

Robber **R**ed is a **r**ascal in Letterland. He's always

Things to do

✿ **Red collection** Let the children paint a large picture Robber Red and display red objects beside it. Encourage the children to wear something red, if possible.

✿ **Rolling** Make a slight slope using a tray or smooth board for rolling various small objects down. The children have to guess which ones will roll. (Sliding does not count.)

✿ **Road safety** Use a road mat, toy cars and toy people for play and for teaching basic road safety.

✿ **'Ring o' ring of roses'** Sing 'Ring o' ring of roses' together. Ask the children why they are singing this song this week and explain that the reason is because we can hear 'RRRobber RRRed's sound' in the song's name.

✿ **Red pictures** Provide different shades of red paper and any other materials for the children to make a variety of red collage pictures. Display them with your red collection (see above).

✿ **Robots** Help the children to construct robots out of junk.

✿ **Robber Red's rainbow** Talk about the colours of the rainbow and ask the children to paint one, with a pot of gold at one end, which, like the rainbow, is forever out of reach.

✿ **Further practice** For extra practice of the letter shape, use the following materials:
– *Lower Case Pictogram Copymasters*: **r**
– *Early Years Handwriting Copymasters*: 18 and 42.
For consolidation of both letter shape and sound use:
– *Early Years Workbook 3*, pages 12-13.

Things to talk about

✿ **Robbing** Think of some things that the rascal Robber Red would take because they start with his sound.

✿ **Favourite foods** Ask if Robber Red would prefer his potatoes baked or roasted, and then let the children suggest some more of his favourite foods, such as raspberries, rolls, rice, radishes, red jelly, raisins, etc.

✿ **Favourite pastimes** Help the children to decide what Robber Red would most enjoy doing. Perhaps he would ride round and round in a racing car or roller skate by the river.

✿ **Rule breaker** Explain that Robber Red is a rule breaker who takes other people's things. Stress that it's not right and that we don't want to be like him!

✿ **Tongue twister** Try saying together the tongue twister 'Round and round the rugged rock the ragged rascal (or perhaps, real rascal) ran.'

Explaining the capital R shape

 Tell the children that when he starts somebody's name, Robber Red takes a big breath and gets bigger. Get them to look at his fat red jumper and his strong running legs and see if they can still recognise him!

---

in **r**eal trouble, so he's always **r**unning away.

Can you make your fingers **r**un like **R**obber **R**ed's two legs? Change your two fingers into two legs. That's **r**ight.

Are you **rrr**eady with your fingers to **r**un fast? Make them **r**un. And again. **R**un, **r**un, **r**un like **R**obber **R**ed.

Session 2: Robber Red's shape and sound
I'm sure you can **r**emember this **r**ascal's name. Yes, it's **R**obber **R**ed. Can you **r**emember some of the things **R**obber **R**ed has taken? Yes, some **r**oller skates and a **r**ed **r**ing.

Let's see *you* use your fingers to make **r**unning legs and **r**un your fingers along like **R**obber **R**ed.

When **R**obber **R**ed **r**uns into words, he makes a growling sound, like this: '**rrr**..., **rrr**..., **rrr**...' *(through closed teeth).* Let's make his sound together, '**rrr**..., **rrr**..., **rrr**...'. Can you hear that growling sound at the beginning of his name, **R**rr**obber R**rr**ed**? That's the sound he makes in words like **rrr**un and **rrr**ed and **rrr**ing and **rrr**adio...yes and **rrr**oller skates.

When we make **R**obber **R**ed's letter, we start at his neck. We go *down* to his leg, back up and *round* that arm. Are you **r**eady? We start at his neck, go *down* to his leg, back up and *round* his arm, and we say the sound, '**rrr**..., **rrr**...', again, '**rrr**..., **rrr**...' for **R**obber **R**ed.

Sammy Snake

Objective

To teach the letter shapes and sound for **s** and **S**.

What you need

Letterland materials

☆ *Early Years Big Picture Code Cards*: Sammy Snake
☆ *Lower Case Pictogram Copymasters*: **s**
☆ *Early Years Handwriting Copymasters*: 19 and 43
☆ *Early Years Workbook 3*: pages 14-15

Other materials

☆ Stocking
☆ Newspaper
☆ Needle and thread
☆ Sponge pads
☆ Green and yellow paint

☆ Pipe cleaners
☆ Pairs of socks
☆ Washing line or string
☆ Pegs

Teaching suggestions

Introducing Sammy Snake

Show the children the picture of Sammy Snake on page 45 of the *ABC Book* and introduce him using **Session 1** from the *Early Years Cassette* as a guide for what to say. Invite one or more children to find and touch Sammy Snake on the *Class Wall Frieze*. Tell them to touch his head and his yellow and green striped tail.

Sammy Snake's letter shape

After **Session 2**, the following handwriting verse, chanted or sung as on the *Handwriting Songs Cassette*, will help in teaching Sammy Snake's letter shape:

Start at Sam's head where he can see.
Stroke down to his tail, oh so care-ful-ly!

Invite one or more children to finger trace Sammy Snake's letter shape on the *ABC Book* or on both sides of the *Early Years Big Picture Code Cards*.

Sammy Snake's sound

This is a simple hissing sound. If a child adds voice instead of whispering it, the result will be 'sssuh', so stress the hiss as a whispered sound. Sammy Snake's song on the *Alphabet Songs Cassette* will help in achieving the correct sound.

Sammy Snake's words

sad	snail
sand	snake
sandals	soap
sausages	socks
school	sound
scissors	soup
seaside	special
seesaw	spider
sister	star
six	start
sky	summer
sleep	sun
small	sweets

Early Years Cassette transcript

Session 1: Introducing Sammy Snake

This time, before I open my book, you have to be *very* quiet because we're going to meet somebody very special. This creature makes a special hissing sound. Are you ready? Be very quiet so you can hear. I'm opening the book carefully and I'm making his sound, '**sss**...'

Did you hear it? Can *you* make it for me? That's right. And who is it making that sound? A snake. Oh, but look at that smiling snake. Do you think you need to be frightened of this snake? No, I don't. Not when he smiles at you like that. Would you like to know what this snake is called?

Things to do

⭐ **Sleeping snakes** Ask the children to pretend to be snakes. They can all lie down on their stomachs and slither and slide like Sammy Snake. Then they can pretend to sleep. Choose two children to stand and take small steps around the sleeping snakes.

⭐ **Sandpit** Suggest that the children draw Sammy Snake's letter in the sand six or seven times and count them.

⭐ **Stocking Sammy** Let the children stuff a stocking with crumpled newspaper. Sew or tie up the end for them. They can use sponge pads of green and yellow paint to make stripes on on it. Their stuffed stocking Sammy can be either displayed or played with.

⭐ **Pipe cleaner Sammys** The children can bend pipe cleaners into **s**-shapes and mount them with glue onto paper, all snakes looking in the Reading Direction. Draw faces and tails with crayons.

⭐ **Sorting socks** Bring in some pairs of socks. Get the children to sort them into matching pairs, then display them on 'Sammy Snake's sock line' with pegs.

⭐ **Further practice** For extra practice of the letter shape, use the following materials:
– *Lower Case Pictogram Copymasters*: **s**
– *Early Years Handwriting Copymasters*: 19 and 43.
For consolidation of both letter shape and sound use:
– *Early Years Workbook 3*, pages 14-15.

Things to talk about

⭐ **Socks** Following on from the sock sorting activity, find out which is the smallest sock, the longest and the widest sock. Ask what kind of socks the children like best and what kind they think Sammy Snake might have, perhaps striped socks. Let them decide how many he would need: one or none?

⭐ **Seaside** Talk about what Sammy Snake might like beginning with his sound at the seaside. Also talk about anything the children themselves enjoy.

⭐ **Sun** Talk about how the sun helps to keep us warm, and makes the flowers grow and open. Warn about the dangers of too much sun. You could try singing 'The sun has got his hat on'.

⭐ **Sausages** Learn the counting rhyme 'Ten fat sausages sizzling in the pan'.

⭐ **Favourite foods** Ask what the children think Sammy Snake might like for a snack. He likes anything starting with his sound, for example, soup, sandwiches, sausage rolls, sweets, spaghetti, strawberries, spiders, even when they are all sandy!

Explaining the capital S shape

 Explain that whenever Sammy Snake has a chance to start an important word, like a name or a word on a sign, he takes a deep breath and gets bigger.

He's **S**ammy **S**nake.

Where is **S**ammy **S**nake? Yes, he's at the seaside. Look he's standing on the **s**and very near to the **s**ea. Do you like going to the **s**easide? Yes, I do. **S**ammy **S**nake looks as if he's having a **s**uper time.

Session 2: Sammy Snake's shape and sound
Do you remember our seaside picture? Who do we **s**ee having a **s**uper time at the **s**easide? Yes, it's **S**ammy **S**nake. Do you remember the **s**ound he makes at the beginning of his name? **S**ay it with me, **S**ammy **S**nake says '**sss**...'.

Wait a minute. Do you hear his **s**pecial **s**ound at the beginning of **s**easide? And where is he standing now? Yes, on the **s**and. Does the word **sand** start with **S**ammy **S**nake's special sound? Listen, **s**and and **s**andcastle start with a hiss, too.

What is the red thing by the **s**andcastle? A **s**pade. Does the word **spade** start with **S**ammy **S**nake's special sound? Yes, it does. Oh, **S**ammy **S**nake loves being by the **s**easide and he loves making **s**andcastles and playing on the **s**and.

Let's **s**ay his sound while we make his letter. We're going to start by his head, go *all* the way *round* his body and *down* to his tail. Ready?

Start by his head, go *round* his body and *down* to his tail and let's say '**sss**...' together. That's **S**ammy **S**nake at the seaside.

Ticking Tess

Objective

To teach the letter shapes and sound for **t** and **T**.

What you need

Letterland materials

☆ *Early Years Big Picture Code Cards*: Ticking Tess
☆ *Lower Case Pictogram Copymasters*: **t**
☆ *Early Years Handwriting Copymasters*: 20 and 44
☆ *Early Years Workbook 4*: pages 2-3

Other materials

☆ Long cardboard tubes
☆ Coloured cellophane
☆ Teddy shapes
☆ Small paper circles or buttons
☆ Buttons
☆ Shoe or egg boxes
☆ Toy train set
☆ Bread for making toast or mini toasts
☆ Toy telephone
☆ Clock face

Teaching suggestions

Introducing Ticking Tess

Show the children the picture of Ticking Tess on page 47 of the *ABC Book* and introduce her using **Session 1** from the *Early Years Cassette* as a guide for what to say. Invite one or more children to find and touch Ticking Tess on the *Class Wall Frieze*. Ask them to touch her head, toes and telephone.

Ticking Tess' letter shape

After **Session 2**, the following handwriting verse, chanted or sung as on the *Handwriting Songs Cassette*, will help in teaching Ticking Tess' shape:

> Tall as a tower make Ticking Tess stand.
> Go from head to toe,
> and then from hand to hand.

Invite one or more children to finger trace Ticking Tess' letter shape on the *ABC Book* or on both sides of the *Early Years Big Picture Code Cards*.

Ticking Tess' sound

The children need to avoid saying 'tuh' by whispering this sound. To help them, ask them to touch the top of their mouths with their tongues. Then they can just *start* to say, 'Ticking Tess'. Ticking Tess' song on the *Alphabet Songs Cassette* will help them to achieve the correct sound.

Ticking Tess' words

table	tiny
tall	top
tap	toy
tea	tractor
teddy	train
telephone	tree
telescope	trousers
tell	true
ten	turn
tent	twice

Early Years Cassette transcript

Session 1: Introducing Ticking Tess
Here's a very **t**all person with a **t**elephone in her hand. Can you see her **t**elephone? She's pressing the buttons. I think she's going to **t**elephone somebody. Her name is **T**icking **T**ess. Her office is high up above the **t**ree **t**ops in a very **t**all **t**ower. If you look out of the window, you will see how **t**iny everything looks down below.

Look! **T**icking **T**ess has a **t**elephone in one hand and a long **t**ube in the other hand. Does anybody know what you do with this long **t**ube? That's right. You look through it. It's called a **t**elescope. And if you look through a **t**elescope, you can see things a long, long way away. If **T**icking **T**ess looks

Things to do

★ **Ticking and turning** Tell the children to tick and turn with outstretched arms like Ticking Tess. Ask them to stand on tiptoe so that they can be tall like Ticking Tess and Tom.

★ **Building towers** Suggest that the children build some tall towers with building bricks. How tall can they make the tower before it tips and topples over?

★ **Tess' telescope** Make telescopes for Ticking Tess with long cardboard tubes from tin foil or kitchen roll. Let the children paint them, or cover them with coloured paper. Fix coloured cellophane (e.g. from sweet wrappers) over the end with elastic bands, and then see how the world looks!

★ **Teddy pictures** Prepare some teddy shapes and provide assorted small circles of paper or buttons. The children can stick on matching circles for eyes, add a nose and three buttons down teddy's tum, and draw his mouth.

★ **Treasure chest** The children can paint, then decorate a small box with a lid (for example, a child's shoe box or an egg box) to be a 'treasure chest' for tiny toys.

★ **Trains, tracks and tunnels** Using model train sets, let the children build trains, tracks and tunnels.

★ **Tea party** Have a tea party or a teddy bear's picnic. Drink pretend tea and serve tiny pieces of real toast. (Ticking Tess loves tea and toast.)

★ **Further practice** For extra practice of the letter shape, use the following materials:
– *Lower Case Pictogram Copymasters*: **t**
– *Early Years Handwriting Copymasters*: 20 and 44.
For consolidation of both letter shape and sound use:
– *Early Years Workbook 4*, pages 2-3.

Things to talk about

★ **Talking to Tess** Hand a toy telephone (or a pretend one) around for the children to talk to Tess. Another child (or you) can be Tess. Suggest that they ask Tess what time it is in Letterland, invite her to tea, or simply chat with her.

★ **Telling the time** This week teach the clock positions for twelve, one and two o'clock.

★ **Counting to ten** Practise counting to ten with the children, or even to twenty. Tell them that Ticking Tess thinks that's terrific. Use **terrific** as your main word of praise during this week.

★ **Toys** Ask each child to tell everyone about a favourite toy, or to talk about a toy that he or she would like to be given.

Explaining the capital T shape

Tell the children that when Tess starts her name (or another), she takes a deep breath and grows so tall that her head disappears in the clouds. We still know it's Tess, however, because we can still see her arms.

---

through her **t**elescope, the **t**rain in the distance will look much bigger and much nearer. So will the **t**rain **t**racks and the **t**rees.

Ticking **T**om works in this **t**all **t**ower, **t**oo. **T**icking **T**om isn't in our picture. He's probably out fixing somebody's **t**elephone or **t**elevision set for them.

I can see **t**wo **t**elephones, can you? There's one in **T**ess' hand and a blue one on the wall. Goodbye **T**icking **T**ess.

Session 2: Ticking Tess' shape and sound
How many **t**elephones are there on this page? One, **t**wo. One for **T**icking **T**ess and one for her **t**eam mate, **T**icking **T**om. Listen, their names

start with the same '**t**...' sound. **T**icking **T**ess and **T**icking **T**om. No wonder they like answering **t**elephones, because the word **t**elephone starts with their '**t**...' sound.

Ticking **T**ess has a **t**all letter shape. When we write her letter, we start at her neck, go *all the* way down to her **t**oes, and then we make her arms. Ready? Start at her neck, go *all the way* down to her **t**oes and then make her arms.

While we do it this **t**ime, let's say, '**t**..., **t**...'. We're going to start by her neck, go down to her **t**oes, go across to her **t**elephone hand. And we're going to say, '**t**..., **t**...' because this is the sound **T**icking **T**ess makes in words.

Uppy Umbrella

Objectives

To teach the letter shapes for **u** and **U** and the short vowel sound 'ŭ...', and to introduce the long vowel sound 'ū...'.

What you need

Letterland materials

- ☆ *Early Years Big Picture Code Cards*: Uppy Umbrella and Mr U
- ☆ *Lower Case Pictogram Copymasters*: **u**
- ☆ *Early Years Handwriting Copymasters*: 21 and 45
- ☆ *Early Years Workbook 4*: pages 4-5

Other materials

- ☆ Paper cups
- ☆ Sweets (as many as there are children)

Teaching suggestions

Introducing Uppy Umbrella

Before introducing the short 'ŭ...' sound, it is good idea to revise the short 'ă...', 'ĕ...', 'ĭ...' and 'ŏ...' sounds first. Then show the children the picture of Uppy Umbrella on page 49 of the *ABC Book* and introduce her using **Session 1** from the *Early Years Cassette* as a guide for what to say. Invite one or more children to find and touch Uppy Umbrella on the *Class Wall Frieze*. Talk briefly about the capital **U** and about Mr U in his uniform, if asked (see opposite).

Uppy Umbrella's letter shape

After **Session 2**, the following handwriting verse, chanted or sung as on the *Handwriting Songs Cassette*, will help in teaching Uppy Umbrella's letter shape:

Under the umbrella draw a shape like a cup. Then draw a straight line so it won't tip up.

Invite one or more children to finger trace Uppy Umbrella's letter shape on both sides of the *ABC Book* or on the *Early Years Big Picture Code Cards*.

Uppy Umbrella's sound

Just ask the children to start to say Uppy's name to make her sound. For once there is no 'uh' sound to avoid, because 'uh' *is* her sound. Uppy Umbrella's song on the *Alphabet Songs Cassette* will help in achieving the correct sound.

Uppy Umbrella's words

ugly	underneath	unusual
umbrella	understand	up
unbutton	undone	upside down
uncle	unhappy	upstairs
under	unless	us

Early Years Cassette transcript

Session 1: Introducing Uppy Umbrella

I want you to close your eyes before I open my book. Close your eyes very tightly, and very carefully open your hands. I want you to pretend that it's raining. If it's raining, what would you feel on your hands? That's right. You would feel the raindrops. Lift your hands **up** a little, **up**, **up**, **up**. Can you feel the rain as you pretend that rain is falling on to your fingers? Lift them again. **U**p, **up**, **up**. That's right.

You can open your eyes now. When it really rains, I don't put my hands **up**. I put something else **up**. Can you tell me what else I put **up**? Perhaps if you look at my picture it will help? Yes, I put **up** an **u**mbrella.

Why do I put **up** an **u**mbrella? To keep me dry

Things to do

⭐ **Upside down** The observation game 'Upside down' is brief, but fun to play often, especially during your Uppy Umbrella week. From time to time, secretly turn something in the room upside down. Ask the children, 'What's unusual now?' and let them reply, 'The book (picture, teddy bear, etc.) is upside down.'

⭐ **Under the cup** Hide one sweet under one of the same number of paper cups as there are children. In turn they lift up the cups. The winner sits out and the others cover up their eyes while you hide the next sweet. Repeat until everybody has a sweet.

⭐ **Further practice** For extra practice of the letter shape, use the following materials:
– *Lower Case Pictogram Copymasters*: **u**
– *Early Years Handwriting Copymasters*: 21 and 45. For consolidation of both letter shape and sound use:
– *Early Years Workbook 4*, pages 4-5.

Things to talk about

⭐ **Up** Ask the children to think about the word **up**. We get up out of bed, go up the road/hill, climb up trees/stairs, look up, pick up, use up, fix up, hold up, step up, turn up, build up, keep up, mix up, sew up, grow up, wind up, etc. Help everyone to notice how often the word **up** comes up in the course of the week.

⭐ **Under** Think about the word **under** with the children. Ask what we can go under, such as blankets, tables, bridges, trees, the sun, moon, stars, etc.

Explaining the capital U shape

Like everyone else in Letterland, Uppy Umbrella loves starting important words. Like them, all she has to do to get bigger is to take a deep breath. Talk about what it would be like if we could do this too.

Introducing Mr U, the Uniform Man

Show the children the picture of Mr U, the Uniform Man, on either the *Class Wall Frieze* or on the *Early Years Big Picture Code Cards*. Explain that Mr U has the important job of looking after all the umbrellas in Letterland. He must be important, as he always wears a uniform.

Mr U's words

unicorn
uniform
united
use
useful

---

so that the rain falls on the umbrella. Then it doesn't fall on my hands and it doesn't fall on my head.

Look at our lovely Letterland umbrella. Can you see her colours? Let's point to the colours. There's red, blue, yellow, green, red. What a lovely umbrella. We call her **U**ppy **U**mbrella because we put her **up** when it rains. Can you say her name with me? **U**ppy **U**mbrella!

Session 2: Uppy Umbrella's shape and sound
Shall we hold out our hands again and pretend that it's raining? What do we need for the rain? Yes, an umbrella. Let's find our Letterland umbrella. Can you remember her name? Her name is **U**ppy **U**mbrella.

Uppy **U**mbrella says 'ŭ..., ŭ..., ŭ...' for

umbrella, and 'ŭ...' for up. Let's pretend to put her **up** while we say her 'ŭ...' sound. Have your hand ready holding the umbrella. Press the button, push it **up** and we say 'ŭ...' for **U**ppy **U**mbrella.

Let's do it again. Hold the umbrella, press the button and push it **up** while we make her 'ŭ...' sound.

Her letter shape is her handle. Can you see? Are you ready to make her letter shape? We're going to start at the top by her umbrella. We're going to go *down* under, go *up* to the top and down again to stop it tipping over. Let's do it again while we say **U**ppy **U**mbrella's 'ŭ...' sound. Start at the top by her umbrella. Go down *under*, and *up* to the top and *down* again, and we say 'ŭ...' for **U**ppy **U**mbrella.

Vase of Violets

Objective

To teach the letter shapes and sound for **v** and **V**.

What you need

Letterland materials

☆ *Early Years Big Picture Code Cards*: Vase of Violets
☆ *Lower Case Pictogram Copymasters*: **v**
☆ *Early Years Handwriting Copymasters*: 22 and 46
☆ *Early Years Workbook 4*: pages 6-7

Other materials

☆ Violet and green tissue paper
☆ Pipe cleaners
☆ Vegetables
☆ Modelling dough
☆ Vanilla pod
☆ Vanilla ice cream
☆ African violet or real violets
☆ Velvet and other contrasting fabrics
☆ Toy vans

Teaching suggestions

Introducing Vase of Violets

Show the children the picture of the Vase of Violets on page 51 of the *ABC Book* and introduce it using **Session 1** from the *Early Years Cassette* as a guide for what to say. Invite one or more children to find and touch Vase of Violets on the *Class Wall Frieze*. Ask them to touch it very carefully, so it won't fall over.

Vase of Violets' letter shape

After **Session 2**, the following handwriting verse, chanted or sung as on the *Handwriting Songs Cassette*, will help in teaching Vase of Violets' letter shape:

Very neatly, start at the top.
Draw down your vase, then up and stop.

Invite one or more children to finger trace Vase of Violets' letter shape on the *ABC Book* or on both sides of the *Early Years Big Picture Code Cards*.

Vase of Violets' sound

The trick here again is to avoid an 'uh' sound, in this case by keeping teeth on lips while prolonging the 'vvv...' sound. Look out for children who substitute 'fff...' for 'vvv...'. Vase of Violets' song on the *Alphabet Songs Cassette* will help children to achieve the correct sound.

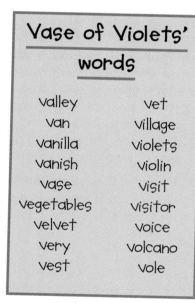

Vase of Violets' words	
valley	vet
van	village
vanilla	violets
vanish	violin
vase	visit
vegetables	visitor
velvet	voice
very	volcano
vest	vole

Early Years Cassette transcript

Session 1: Introducing Vase of Violets

What a lovely **V**ase of **V**iolets! We even call that colour **v**iolet. So the colour is **v**iolet and those flowers are called **v**iolets as well. Can you say the word with me? **V**iolet. Let's say, '**V**ase of **V**iolets.' Ready? '**V**ase of **V**iolets.'

When you say the '**vvv**...' sound, it makes your lips tremble. We call it **v**ibrating. You say it with me. Ready? '**V**vv..., **v**vv..., **V**ase of **V**iolets.' Did you feel your lip **v**ibrating, making that trembly feeling?

These **v**iolets are **v**ery special. They have five

Things to do

⭐ **Making violets** Help to make violets by wrapping violet tissue paper around pipe cleaners for petals. For each violet, tie on five tissue paper leaves (good counting practice). Add the children's names to them. Make a display, perhaps in one or more vases. At the end of the week, everyone can take their violets home with them.

⭐ **Vegetable soup** Ask each child to bring in some vegetables on the day that you do **Session 2**. Let the children watch while you chop up vegetables to make vegetable soup. Encourage them to taste various raw vegetables before they are cooked. Serve the same day, or if need be, cook later and serve the next day.

⭐ **Valleys** Make a model of mountains with modelling dough. Let the children flatten several mountains to make valleys. Then decorate them with 'violets' by sprinkling chopped up coloured paper into them.

⭐ **Vanilla** If possible, show the children a vanilla pod, and let them eat some vanilla ice cream.

⭐ **Vanished!** Before the children arrive, remove one item or piece of furniture that is always in the room. See who can work out what has vanished.

⭐ **Further practice** For extra practice of the letter shape, use the following materials:
– *Lower Case Pictogram Copymasters*: **v**
– *Early Years Handwriting Copymasters*: 22 and 46.
For consolidation of both letter shape and sound use:
– *Early Years Workbook 4*, pages 6-7.

Things to talk about

⭐ **Violets** Bring in a pot of African violets, or real violets if possible. Talk about how different flowers grow in only certain colours, for example, buttercups and dandelions are always yellow. Violets can be bluish or white, but most violets are a shade of purple which we call 'violet' after the flowers themselves.

⭐ **Velvet** Talk about different kinds of cloth. Bring in a piece of velvet for the children to feel and compare with other materials.

⭐ **Voices** Talk about our voices and explore the range of sounds the children can make. Practise both the vowel sounds ('ă...', 'ĕ...', 'ĭ...', 'ŏ...' and 'ŭ...') and the vowel names ('ā...', 'ē...', 'ī...', 'ō...' and 'ū...').

⭐ **Vets** Talk about a vet's job (as an 'animal doctor') and ask if anyone has been to a vet with their own pet.

⭐ **Vans** Talk about the various things that might be carried in a van or who might use one. If available, show the children some toy vans, e.g. a breakdown van, delivery van, etc.

⭐ **Very good** Use **very good** as your main words of praise during your Vase of Violets week.

Explaining the capital V shape

 Ask the children why some vases look bigger than others. Explain to them that in Letterland, children bring them nearer to us to show that the word starting with the big vase is an important word.

---

petals. One, two, at the top. Three, four, five at the bottom.

I can see a little **v**ole nibbling some things in the corner of this picture. What is he nibbling? **V**egetables. Listen. **V**egetables. Did you hear the '**vvv**…' sound that **V**ase of **V**iolets makes at the beginning of that word? **V**egetables, **v**iolets in a **v**ase and a little **v**ole. All these words begin with **V**ase of **V**iolet's letter.

Session 2: Vase of Violets' shape and sound
What a beautiful **v**ase for those **v**iolets to sit in. Let's say the name together. **V**ase of **V**iolets.

Did you feel your lips **v**ibrating when you

made the '**vvv**…' sound for **V**ase of **V**iolets? Let's say it again: **V**ase of **V**iolets.

We can draw that **v**ase. We start at the side, go *down* to the bottom of the **v**ase and back up the other side. Are you ready? Start at the side, go *down* to the bottom, and back up again. And we'll say '**vvv**…' while we do it.

Can you remember how many petals the **v**iolet has? Yes, it has five. One, two at the top, and three, four, fi**v**e at the bottom. We can feel the '**vvv**…' sound **v**ibrating at the end of the word fi**v**e. I'll close our book carefully. I must not knock over the **V**ase of **V**iolets.

Wicked Water Witch

Objective

To teach the letter shapes and sound for **w** and **W**.

What you need

Letterland materials

☆ *Early Years Big Picture Code Cards*: Wicked Water Witch and any short vowel card except **u**
☆ *Lower Case Pictogram Copymasters*: **w**
☆ *Early Years Handwriting Copymasters*: 23 and 47
☆ *Early Years Workbook 4*: pages 8-9

Other materials

☆ Cardboard
☆ Cotton wool
☆ Black sticky tape
☆ One or more candles
☆ Corks
☆ Jar with a lid

Teaching suggestions

Introducing Wicked Water Witch

Show the children the picture of the Wicked Water Witch on page 53 of the *ABC Book* and introduce her using **Session 1** from the *Early Years Cassette* as a guide for what to say. Invite one or more children to find and touch Wicked Water Witch on the *Class Wall Frieze*. Ask the children to also touch both pools of water in her two wells.

Wicked Water Witch's letter shape

After **Session 2**, the following handwriting verse, chanted or sung as on the *Handwriting Songs Cassette*, will help in teaching Wicked Water Witch's letter shape:

> When you draw the Witch's wells,
> where she works her wicked spells,
> whizz down and up and then...,
> whizz down and up again.

Invite one or more children to finger trace the Witch's letter shape on the *ABC Book* or on both sides of the *Early Years Big Picture Code Cards*.

Wicked Water Witch's sound

The children will need to avoid adding an 'uh' sound by keeping their lips pursed until after finishing the sound. Try practising the sound together with a vowel by holding *Early Years Big Picture Code Cards* of **w** and a short vowel side by side. Revise other letters in the same way too. Wicked Water Witch's song on the *Alphabet Songs Cassette* will also help in achieving the correct sound.

Wicked Water Witch's words

walk	wax	win
want	we	wind
warm	week	window
wash	well	winter
water	wet	wish
wave	whale	with
way	what	word

Early Years Cassette transcript

Session 1: Introducing Wicked Water Witch
Well, look who has fallen into the **w**ater. Yes. The **W**itch has fallen into the **w**ater. Oh, how silly! Once, on a **w**inter's day, she **w**ished she was somewhere **w**arm, floating above the **w**aves of a deep blue sea, but her **w**ish didn't **w**ork.

What happened? Yes, she fell into the **w**ater. Look at our picture. **W**as it a **w**arm day? Oh, no! It was a cold **w**inter's day. I can see the snow. Poor **W**ater **W**itch. She's fallen into her two **w**ells. Now she **w**ill be soaking **w**et.

I can see something pink in the corner. **W**hat

Things to do

☆ **Wave patterns** Cut out a cardboard 'comb' for the children to make wavy patterns with, using a plateful of finger paints.

☆ **Winter pictures** The children can stick white paper hills and cotton wool snowmen on to coloured paper to make winter scenes. Add a window frame to them using black tape.

☆ **Wax beetles** Beforehand, drip drops of candle wax onto paper to make raised blobs. The children can then add six legs and eyes with paint or crayons to make wax beetles.

☆ **Whale race** The children can pretend to be the wind and blow cork 'whales' across a bowl of water to see which one wins.

☆ **Sinking or floating?** Put a closed empty jar into a bowl of water to see if it floats. First ask the children if it will sink. Add some water and ask if it will still float. Find out together how much water will make it sink. Let them experiment to see what else will sink or float.

☆ **Further practice** For extra practice of the letter shape, use the following materials:
– *Lower Case Pictogram Copymasters*: **w**
– *Early Years Handwriting Copymasters*: 23 and 47. For consolidation of both letter shape and sound use:
– *Early Years Workbook 4*, pages 8-9.

Things to talk about

☆ **Winners and losers** Talk about being good winners and good losers, and how to do it.

☆ **Days of the week** Find out if everyone knows the names of all seven days of the week. Learn them off by heart together. Ask which day of the week will be the Water Witch's favourite (Wednesday).

☆ **Wishing** Tell the children that the Water Witch wishes that her hair was white because the word **white** begins with her sound. Ask what they would like if they could make a wish.

☆ **Road signs** Suggest that the children look out for 'water wells' on road signs. Describe the GIVE WAY sign and explain where to find such signs.

☆ **Favourite foods** Help the children to think of the Water Witch's favourite foods, such as waffles and wine gums.

Explaining the capital W shape

Explain that when the Wicked Water Witch takes a deep breath, her letter gets bigger. It even holds more water! She always makes her letter bigger when she has a chance to start an important word, like somebody's name.

---

is it? Shall I tell you? It's a windmill. **W**hat makes the sails go round on the windmill? Yes, the **w**ind does.

What would happen to the windmill on a warm day, when there's no **w**ind at all? The sails **w**ould be still, **w**ouldn't they? They only move round **w**hen the **w**ind blows them.

Do you think the **w**ind helped to blow the **W**ater **W**itch into her **w**ater **w**ells?

Session 2: Wicked Water Witch's shape and sound

Can you remember the Letterland **w**itch's name? Yes, **w**e call her the **W**ater **W**itch. Can you hear her '**www**...' sound **w**hen I say her name?

Ww**w**ater **W**w**w**itch. Look, her letter holds the **w**ater in her **w**ater wells, **w**ith one pool on each side.

Our **W**ater **W**itch makes a sound in **w**ords which is like the **w**ind blowing. '**W**ww...', she says, '**W**ww..., **www**..., **www**...'. Can you make the **W**w**w**ater **W**w**w**itch's **w**indy sound?

Let's see if **w**e can dra**w** the side of her **w**ells. Are you ready? **W**e start at this side by her red **w**ellington boots. **W**e go *down*, up, and *down*, up again. Let's try once more and **w**e'll say her sound **w**hile **w**e do it. Start by her **w**ellingtons, go *down*, up, and *down*, up **w**hile **w**e make the **W**ater **W**itch's '**www**...'.

Max and Maxine

Objective

To teach the letter shapes and sound for **x** and **X**.

What you need

Letterland materials

☆ *Early Years Big Picture Code Cards*: Max and Maxine
☆ *Lower Case Pictogram Copymasters*: **x**
☆ *Early Years Handwriting Copymasters*: 24 and 47
☆ *Early Years Workbook 4*: pages 10-11

Other materials

☆ Sandpaper
☆ White or yellow wax crayons or candles
☆ 5 large cardboard boxes
☆ Icing sugar
☆ Cake ingredients

Teaching suggestions

Introducing Max and Maxine

Show the children the picture of Max and Maxine on page 55 of the *ABC Book* and introduce them using **Session 1** from the *Early Years Cassette* as a guide for what to say. Invite one or more children to find and touch Max and Maxine on the *Class Wall Frieze* and to touch their capital letter shape, as well.

Max and Maxine's letter shape

After **Session 2**, the following handwriting verse, chanted or sung as on the *Handwriting Songs Cassette*, will help in teaching Max and Maxine's letter shape:

> Fix two sticks, to look like this.
> That's how to draw a little kiss.

Invite one or more children to finger trace Max and Maxine's letter shape on the *ABC Book* or on both sides of the *Early Years Big Picture Code Cards*.

Max and Maxine's sound

This sound is tricky because it is really two sounds: 'k' + 's'. That is why it helps to whisper the word 'k…ss'. Try whispering all the words in **Max and Maxine's words** with the children. Max and Maxine's song on the *Alphabet Songs Cassette* will also help in achieving the correct sound.

Max and Maxine's words

box	fox	next	sixty
exit	mix	six	taxi
fix	mixture	sixteen	wax

Early Years Cassette transcript

Session 1: Introducing Max and Maxine
These two good friends go to the same school and they're cousins. The boy is called **Max** and the girl is called **Maxine**. Do you know anyone called **Max**? Can you say 'Max' for me? Max. Do you know anyone called Maxine? Can you say 'Maxine'? Maxine.

Just behind Max there's a lovely brown fox. Can you see the fox looking at Max? Is he looking at you as well?

Max and Maxine are very good friends. When they give each other birthday cards, do you know what they write on the birthday card? They write

Things to do

✰ **X pictures** The children can help to cut strips of sandpaper and glue them in six **x**-shapes on to a piece of card or stiff paper. They can shut their eyes and finger trace **x**'s while counting to six and then open their eyes and point as they say 'kss' six times.

✰ **Wax resist** Help the children to draw **x**-shapes on pieces of paper with a white or yellow wax crayon (or a candle). Then let them paint the paper completely with watery black or blue paint. Watch together as the **x**'s disappear under the paint and then appear again.

✰ **Boxes** Tape five large cardboard boxes together in an **x**-shape after cutting holes on four sides of the central box and also in the adjoining outer boxes. The children can crawl through the crossing tunnels.

✰ **Crossroads** Using a road mat, show the children how to be careful at crossroads, with the help of toy cars and toy people. Ask them to see how many crossroads they can count on the mat.

✰ **Kisses** Help to make a card to parents, and then to 'write' in it with love and kisses (**XXX**).

✰ **Cookery** Help the children to ice **x**'s on to biscuits as kisses. They could also help to mix a cake.

✰ **Further practice** For extra practice of the letter shape, use the following materials:
  – *Lower Case Pictogram Copymasters*: **x**
  – *Early Years Handwriting Copymasters*: 24 and 47.
  For consolidation of both letter shape and sound use:
  – *Early Years Workbook 4*, pages 10-11.

Things to talk about

✰ **EXIT signs** Make an EXIT sign to put over the door which the children use to leave the building. Talk about other places where they might look out for this sign, such as in shops, cinemas, etc. Get them to listen to Max and Maxine's sound just after Eddy Elephant's sound in this word. Explain that Max and Maxine's letter does not appear in many words. The children will have to look out for it inside words and at the end of words, because very few start with it. Find some words together, such as **fox**, **wax**, **fix** or even **chicken pox**!

✰ **Taxis** Talk about taxis and how or where you might find one. Explain that people might use a taxi if they do not have a car, or do not live near public transport. Ask if anyone has ridden in a taxi. Then try making up a story about Max and Maxine taking a taxi. They could see some **x**-words on their taxi ride, such as a **fox** crossing the road, somebody carrying **six** or **sixteen** boxes, a person **fixing** a car, etc.

✰ **Foxes** Max and Maxine have a pet fox. Talk about foxes, e.g. where they live, what they eat, etc. Explain that a female fox is called a **vixen**.

Explaining the capital X shape

Ask the children if they can guess how Max and Maxine make their letter look bigger, like many of their friends in Letterland. (They just take a deep breath.)

---

down kisses! Did you know that their letter shape means a kiss? It does!

On this card which Maxine is giving to Max she has put six kisses because Max is six years old. Happy birthday, Max.

Session 2: Max and Maxine's shape and sound

Can you remember the name of these cousins? Yes, they are Max and Maxine. And when they send a birthday card to each other, what do they put on the birthday card? Kisses!

Do you know the special sound of this letter is almost like a kiss sound. You listen, '**kss**…, **kss**…, **kss**…'.

When we write it, we start at Max's head, but we go *down* to Maxine's feet. And then we start at Maxine's head, and whose feet do we go down to? Max's. That's right. Their letter is just two straight lines that cross over.

Let's say Max and Maxine's sound while we make their letter shape, shall we? Ready? Start by Max's head, '**kss**…, **kss**…'. Well done. So Max and Maxine send the '**kss**…, **kss**…' sound to each other.

What was this creature? Yes. He's a fox. Listen, that word **fox** has the same '**kss**…' sound at the end. Let's draw Max and Maxine's letter in the air while we say '**kss**…'.

Yellow Yo-yo Man

Objective

To teach the letter shapes and sound for **y** and **Y**.

What you need

Letterland materials

☆ *Early Years Big Picture Code Cards*: Yellow Yo-yo Man, Eddy Elephant and Sammy Snake
☆ *Lower Case Pictogram Copymasters*: **y**
☆ *Early Years Handwriting Copymasters*: 25 and 48
☆ *Early Years Workbook 4*: pages 12-13

Other materials

☆ Yellow tissue paper
☆ Cardboard circles
☆ String
☆ Polystyrene trays or corks
☆ Straws or cocktails sticks
☆ Yellow sack or bag
☆ Different flavoured yogurts
☆ Raw and cooked eggs

Teaching suggestions

Introducing Yellow Yo-yo Man

Show the children the picture of Yellow Yo-yo Man on page 57 of the *ABC Book* and introduce him using **Session 1** from the *Early Years Cassette* as a guide for what to say. Invite one or more children to find and touch Yo-yo Man on the *Class Wall Frieze*. Ask a child to find and touch the yellow yo-yos in his sack.

Yo-yo Man's letter shape

After **Session 2**, the following handwriting verse, chanted or sung as on the *Handwriting Songs Cassette*, will help in teaching Yo-yo Man's letter shape:

> You first make the yo-yo sack
> on the Yo-yo Man's back,
> and then go down to his toes
> so he can sell his yo-yos.

Invite one or more children to finger trace Yo-yo Man's letter shape on the *ABC Book* or on both sides of the *Early Years Big Picture Code Cards*.

Yo-yo Man's sound

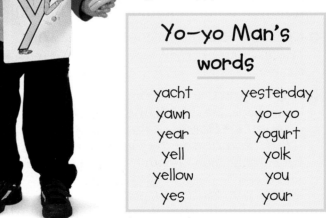

The Yo-yo Man only makes his 'yyy...' sound at the *start* of words. If asked, explain that at the *end* of words like **my,** he says, 'ī...' for Mr I, and for words like **Daddy**, he says 'ē...' for Mr E. The Yo-yo Man's song on the *Alphabet Songs Cassette* will help in achieving the correct sound.

Set out the *Early Years Big Picture Code Cards* to spell the word **yes** and teach this word to the children by showing how their sounds blend together: 'yyye...sss'.

Yo-yo Man's words

yacht	yesterday
yawn	yo-yo
year	yogurt
yell	yolk
yellow	you
yes	your

Early Years Cassette transcript

Session 1: Introducing Yellow Yo-yo Man
What a smart man. He's all dressed in **y**ellow. What has he got on his back? Is it a sack? I wonder what is inside that sack? It's not a ball. It's not even a ball on a string. It looks like a ball on a string, doesn't it? It has a very special name. It's called a **yo-yo**.

If **y**ou are very clever, **y**ou can make a **yo-yo** go up and down the string, up and down. That's a **yo-yo**. I'm not very good at making the **yo-yo** go up and down the string. But this man is.

We call this man the **Y**ellow **Y**o-**y**o Man. He

Things to do

☆ **Yellow collection**
Ask everyone to bring in as many objects as possible that are yellow. Display them under a big painting of the Yo-yo Man or a collage made by crumpling and sticking on yellow tissue paper. Ask the children to try to wear something yellow during the week.

☆ **Hunt the yo-yos** Help the children to make simple yo-yos made out of cardboard discs on string. Then play 'Hunt the yo-yos' with only a little piece of string showing as a clue as to where to find each one.

☆ **Yachts** Help the children to make yachts from junk, such as polystyrene trays, with masts from drinking straws and paper sails, or cocktail sticks with a small paper sail stuck into corks. Then they can race the yachts across a water tray, blowing hard.

☆ **Yo-yo Man mime** The children can take turns in miming the Yo-yo Man getting up, yawning, getting dressed, filling his sack with yo-yos, setting off yelling 'Yyyo-yos for sale', and selling some to everyone.

☆ **Food** Suggest the children try some different yogurt flavours.

☆ **Further practice** For extra practice of the letter shape, use the following materials:
– *Lower Case Pictogram Copymasters*: y
– *Early Years Handwriting Copymasters*: 25 and 48.
For consolidation of both letter shape and sound use:
– *Early Years Workbook 4*, pages 12-13.

Things to talk about

☆ **Yesterday** Make a list of things that you have done today. Go over them the next day stressing how they all happened yesterday. Repeat on several days.

☆ **Year** Tell the children that there are 365 days in the year. Ask them individually how many years old they are and how old their brother, sister, dog is, etc. Talk about the seasons that make up the year.

☆ **Egg yolks** Look at egg yolks together and compare a cooked yolk with an uncooked yolk.

☆ **Young** Talk about young and old. Ask the children if they know someone very young or if there is someone younger than them in the family. Find out the names of young animals together, e.g. puppy, kitten, calf, lamb, etc.

☆ **Yaks** Many alphabets use a picture of a yak to represent the initial sound of **y**. Link the yak to the Yo-yo Man by explaining that he enjoys visiting the yaks at the Letterland zoo. The zoo keeper lets him feed the yaks there with special yellow yak food.

☆ **Yawning** Ask the children what we usually do every evening that the Yo-yo Man does as well. Explain that yawning can be catching. Get everyone to pretend to yawn and then see if they find themselves yawning again for real.

Explaining the capital Y shape

Tell the children that when the Yo-yo Man has a chance to be in an important word, he quickly empties out some of his yo-yos (which are heavy) so that he can step lightly up on to the line to show how important that word is.

---

has loads of **yo-yo**s in his sack and he's dressed in **y**ellow. Let's look out for the **Y**ellow **Yo-yo** Man's letter in words.

Goodbye for now, **Y**ellow **Yo-yo** Man. We'll see **y**ou again soon. Goodbye, **Y**ellow **Yo-yo** Man.

Session 2: Yellow Yo-yo Man's shape and sound

Do **y**ou remember the name of this **y**ellow thing on a string? **Y**es, it's a **yo-yo**. Our friend here is called the **Y**ellow **Yo-yo** Man. Look at his long **y**ellow letter. Shall we make his letter?

Start at the outside of his sack, go *right* down it, *up* to his neck and *down* his long **y**ellow legs. Ready?

Let's do it again and make his sound while we do it. It's a very quiet sound, '**yyy**…, **yyy**…' for **Yo-yo** Man.

Start at the outside of his sack, go *right* down, *up* to his neck and *down* his long **y**ellow legs and say '**yyy**…, **yyy**…' for **Yo-yo** Man. '**Yyy**…' for **y**ellow and '**yyy**…' for **yo-yo**.

Oh, there's a special boat on the sea by the **Yo-yo** Man. We can't call it a boat, because it has to start with **Yo-yo** Man's sound. Does anybody know what that special sort of boat is called? That's right. It's a **y**acht. A **y**acht always has big sails like that to catch the wind. **Yacht** starts with **Y**ellow **Yo-yo** Man's '**yyy**…' sound.

Zig Zag Zebra

Objective

To teach the letter shapes and sound for **z** and **Z**.

What you need

Letterland materials

☆ *Early Years Big Picture Code Cards*: Zig Zag Zebra
☆ *Lower Case Pictogram Copymasters*: **z**
☆ *Early Years Handwriting Copymasters*: 26 and 48
☆ *Early Years Workbook 4*: pages 14-15

Other materials

☆ Black and white paper
☆ Small toy animals
☆ Pictures of rare zoo animals
☆ Toy model zoo (if available)
☆ Zips
☆ Toy or model rocket
☆ Orange or lemon
☆ Peeler or zester
☆ Ingredients for cakes or biscuits

Teaching suggestions

Introducing Zig Zag Zebra

Show the children the picture of Zig Zag Zebra on page 59 of the *ABC Book* and introduce her using **Session 1** from the *Early Years Cassette* as a guide for what to say. Invite one or more children to find and touch Zig Zag Zebra on the *Class Wall Frieze*. Ask them how she looks when she starts important words.

Zig Zag Zebra's letter shape

After **Session 2**, the following handwriting verse, chanted or sung as on the *Handwriting Songs Cassette*, will help in teaching Zig Zag Zebra's letter shape:

> Zip along Zig Zag's nose.
> Stroke her neck...,
> stroke her back... Zzzoom!
> Away she goes.

Invite one or more children to finger trace Zig Zag Zebra's letter shape on the *ABC Book* or on both sides of the *Early Years Big Picture Code Cards*.

Zig Zag Zebra's sound

This is an easy sound to learn and is fun to practise. The children may like to make four fingers gallop while they all say 'zzz...' together. Further practice can also be found by listening to Zig Zag Zebra's song on the *Alphabet Songs Cassette*.

Zig Zag Zebra's words

crazy
dizzy
fizzy
lazy
puzzle
zebra
zebra crossing
zero
zip
zoo
zoom

Early Years Cassette transcript

Session 1: Introducing Zig Zag Zebra
Who have I got here? A **z**ebra. This is **Z**ig **Z**ag **Z**ebra. Look at her **z**ig **z**ag body and her **z**ig **z**ag stripes.

    Zig **Z**ag **Z**ebra doesn't live in a park. Where does she live? In a **z**oo.

    I don't often see a **Z**ig **Z**ag **Z**ebra in the road, but I do see something else that is in this picture. Sometimes when I'm trying to cross the road I look for this. What is it? That's right. It's a **z**ebra crossing. I wonder why they call it a **z**ebra

Things to do

⭐ **Zebra crossing** Make a zebra crossing by taping strips of black and white paper together or get the children to paint one. Then use it to practise care in crossing the road. Stress that even with a zebra crossing, they should never cross the road alone and never run into the road.

⭐ **Zoo animals** Ask the children to bring in small toy animals and include pictures of rare zoo animals, if possible. Sort them into zoo animals, farm animals and perhaps also indoor and outdoor pets. If a toy model zoo is available, use it for play activities, or use model farm fences to create enclosures.

⭐ **Zoo play** Mark out and label different areas for zoo animals. Appoint one or several children as 'zoo keepers'. Let the other children choose which animals to be. The 'zoo keepers' can mime feeding the animals.

⭐ **Zebra's tail** Play 'Pin the tail on the zebra' (instead of the donkey).

⭐ **Being zebras** Help the children to make black and white ears from card or stiff paper and attach them to card headbands. They can also make and wear black and white tails. The 'zebras' can gallop about outside, practising 'zzz...' sounds.

⭐ **Further practice** For extra practice of the letter shape, use the following materials:
– *Lower Case Pictogram Copymasters*: **z**
– *Early Years Handwriting Copymasters*: 26 and 48.
For consolidation of both letter shape and sound use:
– *Early Years Workbook 4*, pages 14-15.

Things to talk about

⭐ **Zebras** Talk about their stripes, where they live, and the kinds of animals that live with them: antelopes, gazelles, wildebeests, lions, leopards, etc.

⭐ **Zips** Talk about how zips work and practise using them on clothes or other items. Point out how the word **zip** and other words, such as **zoom**, **sizzle** and **fizzy** are closely related to the sounds they make. Explain that Zig Zag Zebra loves being in words that come from special sounds!

⭐ **Zero** Talk about the word **zero** and its meaning. Do a countdown together, ten to zero and blast off, if possible with a toy or model rocket.

⭐ **Zest** Scrape lemon or orange peel while explaining that it is also called the **zest**. Use it later in a biscuit dough or cake mixture for baking and eating.

Explaining the capital Z shape

Explain that when Zig Zag Zebra has a chance to start an important word, she takes a deep breath and gets bigger. We don't see her looking big (or small) very often in words, however, because she is very shy.

---

crossing? Of course. It's got the same black and white stripes as our **Z**ig **Z**ag **Z**ebra.

Next time I go out shopping and see a zebra crossing, I'm going to remember **Z**ig **Z**ag **Z**ebra who lives in our Letterland **z**oo.

Oh dear. I wonder who has left that **z**ip bag there on the ground. I hope no-one has lost it. '**Z**ig **Z**ag **Z**ebra, do you know?'

Session 2: Zig Zag Zebra's shape and sound
I know you'll remember our zebra's name. Her black and white stripes and her special shape will remind you. Yes, it's **Z**ig **Z**ag **Z**ebra.

Just look how her letter zig zags when we draw it. I'm going to start by her nose and I'm going to zig zag from her head *right* down to her tail.

Let's do it again. Ready? Start by her nose and zig zag down to her tail.

Do you like doing up zips? I do, and I like to say 'zzzip!' as I zzzip it up. I like saying zzzig zzzag, too. Do you?

Now let's just *start* to say **Z**ig **Z**ag **Z**ebra's name. That's how we can remember the little 'zzz...' sound she makes in words. **Z**ig **Z**ag **Z**ebra says 'zzz...'.

The Alphabet Songs

These songs can be heard on the *Alphabet Songs Cassette*.

Familiar nursery tunes are a popular and effective vehicle for Letterland verses which practise each letter's sound. Before singing a particular song, a leader, who could be the teacher or a child, can hold up the appropriate *Early Years Big Picture Code Card*, plain side first, then the pictogram side, and then announce the character's name. Where a letter has a voiceless sound, i.e. in the case of **c**, **f**, **h**, **k**, **p**, **q**, **s**, **t** and **x**, make sure the children sing it in a whisper.

Annie Apple

(*To the tune of **London bridge is falling down***)

Annie Apple, she says 'ă...'
She says 'ă...', she says 'ă...'
Annie Apple, she says 'ă...'
She belongs to Mr A.

Bouncy Ben

(*To the tune of **Polly put the kettle on***)

Bouncy Ben says 'b...' in words,
Bouncy Ben says 'b...' in words,
Bouncy Ben says 'b...' in words,
before he bounces home.

Clever Cat

(*To the tune of **Merrily we roll along***)

Clever Cat says 'c...' in words,
'c...' in words, 'c...' in words,
Clever Cat says 'c...' in words,
and cuddles close to me.

She also makes another sound,
another sound, another sound.
She also makes another sound.
Just you wait and see.

Dippy Duck

(*To the tune of **Hey, diddle diddle***)

Dippy Duck, Dippy Duck,
we never hear her quack.
She says 'd..., d...' instead.
The little duck dips
and dives about
as the water drips over her head.

Eddy Elephant

(*To the tune of **Oh the grand old Duke of York***)

Here comes Eddy El-e-phant
to talk to you and me.
He just says 'ĕ...', he just says 'ĕ...'
He belongs to Mr E.

Fireman Fred

(*To the tune of **Here we go round the mulberry bush***)

Fireman Fred goes 'fff..., fff..., fff...',
Fireman Fred, Fireman Fred;
Fireman Fred goes 'fff..., fff..., fff...',
fighting fires with foam.

Golden Girl

(*To the tune of* **Merrily we roll along**)

Golden Girl says 'g...' in words,
'g...' in words, 'g...' in words.
Golden Girl says 'g...' in words,
giggling merrily.

Her girlfriend makes another sound,
another sound, another sound.
Her girlfriend makes another sound.
Just you wait and see.

Hairy Hat Man

(*To the tune of* **The wheels on the bus**)

The Hairy Hat Man whispers 'hhh...',
whispers 'hhh...', whispers 'hhh...'
The Hairy Hat Man whispers 'hhh...'
He never talks out loud.

Impy Ink

(*To the tune of* **London Bridge is falling down**)

Impy Ink says 'ĭ...' in words,
'ĭ...' in words, 'ĭ...' in words.
Impy Ink says 'ĭ...' in words.
He belongs to Mr I.

Jumping Jim

(*To the tune of* **Old MacDonald had a farm**)

Jumping Jim says 'j...' in words,
as he jumps along.
Jumping Jim says 'j...' in words,
as he jumps along.
With a 'j..., j...' here, and a 'j..., j...' there;
here a 'j...', there a 'j...',
everywhere a 'j..., j...'
Jumping Jim says 'j...' in words
as he jumps along.

Kicking King

(*To the tune of* **Merrily we roll along**)

Kicking King says 'k...' in words,
'k...' in words, 'k...' in words,
Kicking King says 'k...' in words,
as he kicks along.

Lamp Lady

(*To the tune of* **Twinkle, twinkle, little star**)

Look, look, look, that lovely light.
It's Lamp Lady's light so bright.
Listen, 'lll...' is what she'll say,
'lll...' for lamp, both night and day.
Look, look, look, that lovely light.
It's Lamp Lady's light so bright.

Munching Mike

(*To the tune of **Humpty Dumpty***)

'Mmm...', that monster Munching Mike.
My, he has an appetite.
'Mmm...', he hums contentedly,
munching mouthfuls merrily.

Naughty Nick

(*To the tune of **Sing a song of sixpence***)

Naughty Nick is noisy,
banging all around.
But he's not a bad boy
when he makes his sound.
Listen, can you hear him,
'Nnn...' he says all day.
Even when he's banging nails,
that's what you'll hear him say.

Oscar Orange

(*To the tune of **Polly put the kettle on***)

Oscar Orange, he says 'ŏ...',
Oscar Orange, he says 'ŏ...',
Oscar Orange, he says 'ŏ...'
He belongs to Mr O.

Poor Peter

(*To the tune of **The wheels on the bus***)

Poor, poor Peter just says 'p...',
just says 'p...', just says 'p...',
Poor, poor Peter just says 'p...',
his poor ears droop.

Quarrelsome Queen

(*To the tune of **Here we go round the mulberry bush***)

Quarrelsome Queen says 'qu...' in words,
'qu...' in words, 'qu...' in words.
Quarrelsome Queen says 'qu...' in words.
She *must* have her umbrella.

Robber Red

(*To the tune of **Three blind mice***)

Rob-ber Red, Rob-ber Red.
See how he runs. See how he runs.
He rrreally makes a growling sound.
He's always heard, but he's never found.
Have you ever seen such a rascal around
'Rrr..., rrr..., rrr...'

Sammy Snake

(*To the tune of **Sing a song of sixpence***)

Sammy Snake says 'sss...' in words,
hissing all the time.
Sammy Snake says 'sss...' in words,
hissing all the time.
Hissing with a 'sss..., sss...',
hissing with a 'sss...'
Sammy Snake says 'sss...' in words,
he's hissing all the time.

Ticking Tess

(*To the tune of **Old MacDonald had a farm***)

Ticking Tess says 't...' in words,
ticking all the time.
Ticking Tess says 't...' in words,
ticking all the time.

With a 't..., t...' here and a 't..., t...' there;
here a 't...', there a 't...',
everywhere a 't..., t...'
Ticking Tess says 't...' in words,
ticking all the time.

Uppy Umbrella

(*To the tune of* **Here we go round the mulberry bush**)

Uppy Umbrella says 'ŭ...' in words,
'ŭ...' in words, 'ŭ...' in words.
Uppy Umbrella says 'ŭ...' in words.
She belongs to Mr U.

Vase of violets

(*To the tune of* **London's burning**)

Vase of Violets, Vase of Violets.
Very pretty, very pretty.
'Vvv..., vvv...'; 'vvv..., vvv...';
Pour on water, pour on water.

Wicked Water Witch

(*To the tune of* **Polly put the kettle on**)

Wicked Water Witch says 'www...',
Wicked Water Witch says 'www...',
Wicked Water Witch says 'www...'
in all her words.

Max and Maxine

(*To the tune of* **Old MacDonald had a farm**)

Now let's whisper, whisper 'k-ss',
whisper, whisper 'k-ss'.
Now let's whisper, whisper 'k-ss',
whisper, whisper 'k-ss'.
With a 'k-ss', 'k-ss' here and a 'k-ss',
'k-ss' there;
here a 'k-ss', there a 'k-ss',
everywhere a 'k-ss', 'k-ss'.
Now let's whisper, whisper 'k-ss',
whisper, whisper 'k-ss'.

Yo-yo Man

(*To the tune of* **Baa, baa, black sheep**)

Yo-yo Man says 'y...' in words.
Yyyes sir, yes sir, 'y...' in words.
Yellow yo-yos he will sell,
and work for other men as well.

Zig Zag Zebra

(*To the tune of* **Humpty Dumpty**)

Zig Zag Zebra is very shy.
Saying 'zzz...' while zzzipping by.
Zebras often seem to be shy,
but we'll never really know why.

The Handwriting Songs

These songs can be heard on the *Handwriting Songs Cassette*.
Words by Lyn Wendon and Vivien Stone

Annie Apple

At the leaf begin.
Go round the apple this way.
Then add a line down,
so Annie won't roll away.

Bouncy Ben

Brush down Ben's big, long ears.
Go up and round his head
so his face appears!

Clever Cat

Curve round Clever Cat's face to begin.
Then gently tickle her under her chin.

Dippy Duck

Draw Dippy Duck's back. Go round her tum.
Go up to her head. Then down you come!

Eddy Elephant

Ed has a headband. Draw it and then
stroke round his head
and his trunk to the end.

Fireman Fred

First draw Fred's helmet.
Then go down his clothes.
Give him some arms
so he can hold his hose.

Golden Girl

Go round Golden Girl's head.
Go down her golden hair.
Then curve to make her swing
so she can sit there.

Hairy Hat Man

Hurry from the Hat Man's head
down to his heel on the ground.
Go up and bend his knee over,
so he'll hop while he makes his sound.

Impy Ink

Inside the ink bottle draw a line.
Add an inky dot. That's fine!

Jumping Jim

Just draw down Jim, bending his knees.
Then add the one ball
which everyone sees.

Kicking King

Kicking King's body is a straight stick.
Add his arm, then his leg, so he can kick!

Lucy Lamp Lady

Lamp Lady looks like one long line.
Go straight from head to foot
and she's ready to shine!

Munching Mike

Make Munching Mike's back leg first,
then his second leg, and third,
so he can go munch-munching in a word.

Naughty Nick

'Now bang my nail,' Naughty Nick said.
'Go up and over around my head.'

Oscar Orange

On Oscar Orange start at the top.
Go all the way round him, and...then stop.

Poor Peter

Pat Poor Peter properly.
First stroke down his ear,
then up and round his face
so he won't shed a tear.

Quarrelsome Queen

Quickly go round the Queen's cross face.
Then comb her beautiful hair into place.

Robber Red

Run down Robber Red's body.
Go up to his arm and his hand.
Then watch out for this robber
roaming round Letterland.

Sammy Snake

Start at Sam's head where he can see.
Stroke down to his tail, oh so care-ful-ly!

Ticking Tess

Tall as a tower make Ticking Tess stand.
Go from head to toe,
and then from hand to hand.

Uppy Umbrella

Under the umbrella
draw a shape like a cup.
Then draw a straight line
so it won't tip up.

Vase of Violets

Very neatly, start at the top.
Draw down your vase, then up and stop.

Wicked Water Witch

When you draw the Witch's wells,
where she works her wicked spells,
whizz down and up and then...,
whizz down and up again.

Max and Maxine

Fix two sticks, to look like this.
That's how to draw a little kiss.

Yo-yo Man

You first make the yo-yo sack
on the Yo-yo Man's back,
and then go down to his toes
so he can sell his yo-yos.

Zig Zag Zebra

Zip along Zig Zag's nose.
Stroke her neck..., stroke her back...
Zzzoom! Away she goes.

The Letterlanders

Annie Apple

Bouncy Ben

Clever Cat

Dippy Duck

Eddy Elephant

Fireman Fred

Golden Girl

Hairy Hat Man

Impy Ink

Jumping Jim

Kicking King

Lucy Lamp Lady

Munching Mike

Naughty Nick

Oscar Orange

Poor Peter

Quarrelsome Queen

Robber Red

Sammy Snake

Ticking Tess

Uppy Umbrella

Vase of Violets

Wicked Water Witch

Max and Maxine

Yellow Yo-yo Man

Zig Zag Zebra

Letter to parents

Dear Parent/Guardian,

As part of our language teaching, we will be introducing your child to the alphabet, using Letterland. We feel that Letterland is a well established and successful system for teaching children to read and write and meets the required curriculum guidelines.

 Letter shapes and sounds are abstract and often hard for children to learn. In Letterland, letters become friendly 'pictogram' characters. For example, the pictogram character for the letter **a** is Annie Apple.

Your child will learn about the characters which make up the Letterland alphabet. These characters help your child to know and understand letter shapes and sounds. Don't be surprised if your child comes home full of talk about Annie Apple, Clever Cat or the Hairy Hat Man. Show an interest in the characters, even if you don't understand what your child is talking about just yet!

Please help us in this adventure in the following ways:

☆ A letter name is quite different from the sound a letter makes, so try to avoid using the traditional 'aee, bee, cee' letter names at this stage. If your child already knows the alphabet names, just give them a rest for now. The Letterland names are easier and more useful, so you might like to start using them yourself, too, when you talk about letters with your child.

☆ We will be introducing both capital and small letters at the same time. However, in handwriting, please help us to emphasise the small letters first (**a-z**), since these are the most needed shapes. Use capital letters for the beginning of names only.

☆ Remember that holding the pencil correctly and forming letters in the right sequence is more important than neat writing at this stage.

If you would like more information on using Letterland with your child, we will be happy to talk to you about it. You might also be interested to know that a *Letterland Parent's Guide* is available in the shops.

We are looking forward to introducing your child to the world of Letterland and we hope you will join in the fun and the learning with your child at home.

Thank you for your help.